Life, Death
and the Things
That Matter!

Ian J. Drucker

WESTBOW
PRESS®
A DIVISION OF THOMAS NELSON
& ZONDERVAN

Scriptures taken from the Holy Bible, New International
Version®, NIV®. Copyright © 1973, 1978, 1984, 2011 by
Biblica, Inc.™ Used by permission of Zondervan. All rights
reserved worldwide. www.zondervan.com. The "NIV" and
"New International Version" are trademarks registered in the
United States Patent and Trademark Office by Biblica, Inc.™

This book is a work of non-fiction. Unless otherwise noted, the author
and the publisher make no explicit guarantees as to the accuracy of
the information contained in this book and in some cases, names
of people and places have been altered to protect their privacy.

WestBow Press books may be ordered through
booksellers or by contacting:

WestBow Press
A Division of Thomas Nelson & Zondervan
1663 Liberty Drive
Bloomington, IN 47403
www.westbowpress.com
1 (866) 928-1240

Because of the dynamic nature of the Internet, any web addresses or
links contained in this book may have changed since publication and
may no longer be valid. The views expressed in this work are solely those
of the author and do not necessarily reflect the views of the publisher,
and the publisher hereby disclaims any responsibility for them.

Any people depicted in stock imagery provided by Thinkstock are
models, and such images are being used for illustrative purposes only.
Certain stock imagery © Thinkstock.

ISBN: 978-1-9736-1722-8 (sc)
ISBN: 978-1-9736-1721-1 (e)

Print information available on the last page.

WestBow Press rev. date: 2/01/2018

Contents

Special Acknowledgement

I want to acknowledge the love and support of my dear wife, Marti, in the development of this book. She has been amazing in so many ways. It is difficult to come up with the words to explain how important she is, and has been to me throughout our marriage. But, I will do my best.

Marti is my true love, and my best friend. We have been through so much together, and through it all she has been more than I could have ever hoped for her to be. She has loved me, taken care of me and has blessed my life abundantly. In our ministry efforts, we have worked side-by-side spreading the gospel and teaching the Word of God. I have been so blessed to have such a woman of God as my wife and partner in serving the Lord.

Marti has awesome spirit. She is gentle and kind. She is beautiful inside and out. She has a great sense of humor, and makes me laugh daily. She is forgiving and generous. She has strived to supply everything that I needed, when I needed it. She is a great homemaker, and I truly love her and thank God for that.

Since being diagnosed with high-grade and invasive bladder cancer in January of 2017, she has been with me and for me every step of the way. She has been a secretary, a counselor, a sounding board, a medical researcher and my confidant.

In addition to all of this, Marti encouraged me to write this book. She was concerned that our grandchildren would miss out on the guidance and direction that I had to offer them.

So, thank you so much my sweet wife for being who you are. You are living proof that God gives people exactly what they need, exactly when they need it.

Thank you, Father, for my dear wife!

This book is for any and all who desire to read about and gain insight on the issues of life, death and the things that matter!

In this book I am sharing highlights of what I have learned from years of studying the Bible, from my more than 25 years of Christian life and my more than fifteen years of service as a minister of the gospel at three different congregations. I have poured out my thoughts and beliefs on a number of key subjects, inserting specific Scriptures for clarification on these subjects.

In particular I have in mind concerns for my grandchildren Jacob, Brian and Ella; and my niece's sons (especially Foster - who also calls me Pop-Pop) which have moved me to put these thoughts into words. Therefore, this book is dedicated to them and to the glory of God.

Jacob, Brian, Foster and Ella you may not remember me; but please know that I have and will always love you very much! It is probable that by the time you are able to read and understand this I will be gone. As this cancer consumes my body, the likelihood of my existence in this world diminishes. But fear not, for I am not afraid, because perfect love drives out fear. In the event that I am not able to be with you as you grow, I wanted to make sure that I provided you with the guidance and direction that I know you will need to become everything that God wants you to be. Therefore, I ask that you not only read this book but that you keep it handy throughout your life, with the Holy Bible; and that you use both to lead and guide you in your life and relationships.

In this book I have tried to include key concepts and Scriptures that will be the most helpful to you. Certainly, I could have written many more words. However, I wanted to be somewhat brief to keep you attentive. Not only that, but my intent here is to increase your appetite and inspire you to launch out on your own journey with and for God.

I pray God's blessing upon you as you strive to follow Christ!

First Things First, Understanding and Seeking True Happiness

For a long time in my life I tried to create my own happiness. I want you to know that this was a mistake. There are many reasons why this is wrong, but I want to share some with you.

First of all, I have learned that it is impossible for us to create our own happiness. We are humans, and therefore we are fickle beings. What we want one moment, is not what we want the next. We believe that we know what will make us happy, but we don't. What appeals to us in one instance of time, and in one particular situation, quickly fades. Our desires change so quickly that it is often very difficult to keep up with ourselves. By trying to satisfy the instantaneous desires of our flesh, we may be locking ourselves into painful situations which can become very difficult to escape. So, be very careful regarding what you pursue. Your mind and heart can play tricks on you. I have also learned that happiness is a very misunderstood concept. People try to attain certain things like beauty, wealth, power, status, money and sexual fulfillment believing that such attainments will result in their happiness. This is faulty logic, and such things in and of themselves are incapable of producing happiness. Therefore, never rely on anything or anyone to make you happy.

Secondly, you need to understand that happiness is a very misunderstood term and concept. People grow up reading and hearing stories that end with, "And they lived happily ever after." This is, of course, offered up as the conclusion to the story once the main character has attained the love of their life. The story, however, never addresses these people dealing with the issues and struggles of life. So, know that living happily ever after is not some mystical condition that happens based on getting the mate you want, the job you want, the car you want or anything else that you want in any given moment of time. These may be good things, but they cannot and will not produce long-term happiness in your life. The sooner you grasp a solid understanding of these things, the better you will be and you will be less likely to make a crucial life-long mistake.

I want to say something a little off-track here before I forget. Don't live your life in fear! Don't be so afraid of making a mistake that, even after you have carefully considered and prayed about a decision, you fail to move out and do what needs to be done. Especially if the action is something honorable, charitable, praise-worthy or benefits someone else. Failing to move could result in a mistake as well. Mistakes are made of things that we shouldn't have done, but did; and things that we should have done, but didn't. Also, remember that doing things that benefit others is of great value. Too often when people think of happiness they think only of themselves, and not of anyone else. Do not fall into this trap, or this way of thinking. If you do, you may find yourself lonely and without true love. Furthermore, realize that mistakes can make you a better person. Look for the value that mistakes provide. Mistakes have a way of teaching us things that we will not easily forget. When I was a young boy, in the sixth grade, I told a big lie that caused me great heartache. Okay, I am sure you want to hear the lie. Well, here it is. When my mother remarried, I told some of my classmates that she married a professional (NFL) football player quarterback. This happened after I had watched a Monday Night Football game, and one of the teams had a quarterback with the same exact name as my new step-dad. Being proud that I had a new dad, and wanting others to be proud too, I went to school and circulated the good news of my step-dad being an NFL quarterback. After the good news spread, the teacher confronted me. I am very confident that this teacher knew this was a total lie, but the situation was used as a teaching opportunity. Anyway, I was asked to stay after class one day. I could feel the anxiety within me building. My heart was beating fast. Then, the teacher said it. The kids told what I had said. The teacher asked me if I would ask him (my step-dad) to come in and talk to the class about his job, and what it was like being a professional football player. Immediately, and without hesitation, I replied like a pro myself. I said, "Well I'll ask him, but he is very busy." In my youthfulness I thought this would suffice. It is so interesting how we think more lies can get us out of the lies we have already told. This way of thinking is not limited to children. Many adults fall into the same pit. So, watch your tongue! Well, a few weeks later, the teacher asked me to stay after class again. This time, rather than telling another lie, I spilled my guts. Came clean. Told the truth. Confessed. And boy, did that feel good. Confession is good for the soul. This lesson was invaluable for me. I learned at an early age that telling a lie can lead to a lot of discomfort, pressure and the temptation to tell even more lies. I was blessed by having a wonderful and caring teacher. Incidentally, please value and respect your teachers. They provide you with a tremendous service. The feelings that I had over what I had done were decidedly punishment enough. Learn to and strive to accept accountability and punishment for what you do wrong. This attribute is severely lacking in our culture today. Life is full of challenges, but know that you are up to each challenge that comes along. Don't try to run from your mistakes, you can't outrun them. Rather, face them head-on.

Okay, getting back on-track, know that the sooner you learn that happiness is not contingent upon or generated by outward conditions and circumstances, the more likely you are and the closer you are to finding true and long-lasting happiness. Please learn, believe and understand that the only thing in life that matters is God. That's right, God! Living to please God, living in a relationship with God, living to glorify God and knowing that you are alive and remain so because of God. Anything else is insignificant and meaningless. As Solomon, the writer of Ecclesiastes, put it:

> *"Now all has been heard; here is the conclusion of the matter: Fear God and keep his commandments, for this is the duty of all mankind." (Ecclesiastes 12:13)*

Many people say that they aren't sure about God, but they do believe in a "higher power." This type of statement has confused me for a long time. Such people seem to consider themselves as being super-spiritual, and very enlightened. Love them, as God loves them, but please do not accept their belief, or their way of thinking. God is not some mystical force, or farce for that matter, but rather the creator of all that exists. God is the uncaused first cause. The eternal almighty.

Furthermore, please understand that the God that I am speaking of is God the Father, God the Son (in the person of Jesus, the Christ) and God the Holy Spirit. If this is hard for you to accept, don't feel bad. However, please don't stop seeking truth. I am not telling you to accept what I say without question. That would not be good, or beneficial to you. What I am telling you is to embark on your own journey of faith. Seek and you shall find. Knock and the door will be opened. Ask and you will receive. And let the words of Jesus, the Christ, be the catalyst for your journey. They were for me. In particular, while I had to come to terms with all the things that Jesus said, I was moved by the statement that Jesus made recorded for us in the gospel of John. I was cut to the core when I read that Jesus said,

> *"I am the way and the truth and the life. No one comes to the Father except through me." (John 14:6)*

This went against everything I had believed my entire life, up to the age of 33 years-old. The teachings of Jesus caused me to launch-out on a quest to figure out and determine what I believed, and why I believed it. Especially, in the area of happiness.

I have been on my own faith journey to true happiness, and I hope that you are as well. Explore. Learn. Grow. Keep an open mind. However, keep this in mind. True happiness, lasting joy and unending peace can only come from God, by knowing and obeying Jesus. If you have not yet believed in Jesus, as the Christ and the Son of God; then keep searching. I want you to be with me in heaven, at the appointed time. If your parents don't believe in Jesus, then seek Him on your own. More importantly, however, know that this is what Jesus commands you to do. I am telling you the truth. I would not lie to you about this. Honor your parents in all matters, but not when they are leading you away from God. You must love God, Jesus and the truth more than anyone or anything else, including your parents.

True happiness, joy and life-long peace only come when you have the forgiveness of God. When you know that you are His child, and that He is your heavenly Father. When you have received the Holy Spirit, as you are baptized (going completely under water) into Christ for the forgiveness of your sins. And, by the way, don't let anyone convince you that you do not need to be baptized. The Bible makes it clear that you do. And, that you do so of your own volition once you have heard the gospel (Good News) of Jesus, and believe!

> *He (Jesus) said to them (the disciples), "Go into all the world and preach the gospel to all creation. Whoever believes and is baptized will be saved, but whoever does not believe will be condemned. (Mark 16:15-16)*

Let me also put it like this. I grew up with an incorrect understanding about life. I thought that the goal of my life was to live a happy life. I was wrong. There are many reasons which led to my misunderstanding. The concept begins early with many of us. We hear things and we are subjected to many worldly concepts and views. We read and hear stories when we are little. Very often they end with the phrase, "And they lived happily ever after." So, the myth takes root.

I want to help you develop the correct mindset and understanding about happiness, before you go too far in the wrong direction. Therefore, understand that the erroneous goal of living a happy life comes from the world. It is a worldly worldview. Just think about it. You have probably heard people say, "As long as it makes you happy, it's okay." So, families are crushed by extramarital affairs. People are led down paths of pain and destruction, in their quest for happiness. Satan encourages and incites people to make decisions about doing things based on their ability to bring about their own happiness, and what they perceive will make them happy. This is not what God desires for you. God has a different focus in mind for you. The apostle Peter wrote about this.

> *But just as he who called you is holy, so be holy in all you do; for it is written: "Be holy, because I am holy." (1 Peter 1:15-16)*

Herein lies the issue. God desires for you to be Holy. God desires for you to be pure. God desires for you to be set apart for His use and His glory. God desires for you to be like Him.

Paul identifies this desire of God:

> **Follow God's example, therefore, as dearly loved children... (Ephesians 5:1)**

God wants His children to emulate His characteristics, and follow His example!

Does this mean that God does not want you to be happy? No, absolutely not! What does it mean, then? It means that God desires holiness over happiness. It means that if happiness supersedes holiness in your heart, then you will never achieve either. This is a concept which is difficult for many people to understand and/or accept. It can be a very difficult teaching. The world and our culture teach that you can achieve whatever you want. That you can make your dreams come true. And, that you can make yourself happy!

But, what if what you desire goes against the will of God? What if what you desire is sinful and not holy? These are questions that don't usually get asked. Satan doesn't want you to ask them. Satan would rather you focus on your own desires, even if they go against the Word and will of God. These, of course, are masked or camouflaged with the rationalization that it's all okay, because you are merely doing what is necessary for you to achieve happiness.

I have learned, however, that true happiness comes from knowing that you are living a holy life in the sight of God. True happiness comes from knowing that you are living under the power of the Holy Spirit. True happiness comes from loving God, and being loved by God in and through Christ!

So, in conclusion, I want you to remember that to be truly happy, don't seek happiness. Rather, seek God. The greatest happiness you will ever achieve is to know that you are seeking to live with and for the glory of God every day of your life! When you do this, God will meet all of your needs and provide abundant blessings.

> *But seek first his kingdom and his righteousness, and all these things will be given to you as well. (Matthew 6:33)*

You were created to be in a loving relationship with the One who created you! God sacrificed His Son, Jesus, so that you could have such a relationship, and have it abundantly. Seek to establish a loving relationship with God, in Christ; and once you have it cherish it!

True happiness is achieved by being loved by God, loving God in return and living to please God every day of your life!

The Reality of Life and Death

Every person should develop the correct mindset regarding the reality of life and death. I want to help you with this. There are four aspects of life and death, as follows:

- Physical Life – Alive in physical form
- Physical Death – No longer alive in physical form
- Spiritual Life – Forgiven of sin, and born again by the Holy Spirit
- Spiritual Death – Remaining in and/or dying physically in an unforgiven state

Every person who is alive in the body has Physical Life. Every person who has Physical Life will also experience Physical Death – unless Jesus returns before their Physical Death.

Spiritual Life only occurs when a person is baptized into Christ, and they are born again. The expression born again is applicable because they experience a second birth – a Spiritual Birth. This birth occurs because in baptism a person receives the Holy Spirit of God. They are reborn Spiritually, and raised to a new life. They are raised to life, and in this new life they live to please God. They are able to live a life pleasing to God, because God has put His Spirit into them enabling them to live a life that is pleasing in His sight. In baptism, a person is regenerated (made new) by the Holy Spirit. That is why the Scriptures say:

> *Therefore, if anyone is in Christ, the new creation has come: The old has gone, the new is here! (2 Corinthians 5:17)*

When a person is baptized into Christ they are also united in the death, burial and resurrection of Christ. The same power that raised Jesus from His Physical Death to Physical Life (in His resurrection), is the same power that resurrects people from Spiritual Death to Spiritual Life in the act of baptism. This is why the Scriptures say:

> *...and this water symbolizes baptism that now saves you also—not the removal of dirt from the body but the pledge of a clear conscience toward God. It saves you by the resurrection of Jesus Christ... (1 Peter 3:21)*

Everything pertaining to the Christian faith hinges on the resurrection of Jesus.

So, then, once a person is baptized into Christ they have crossed over from Spiritual Death to Spiritual Life. Even though they may die a Physical Death, they are always alive Spiritually (to God). Spiritual Life is eternal life with the promise of heaven. And your eternal life begins with believing in and obeying the commands of Christ and being baptized. That is why Jesus said:

> *"Very truly I tell you, whoever hears my word and believes him who sent me has eternal life and*

> *will not be judged but has crossed over from death*
> *to life. (John 5:24)*

That is also why Jesus said:

> *"I am the resurrection and the life. The one who*
> *believes in me will live, even though they die;*
> *and whoever lives by believing in me will never*
> *die. (John 11:25-26)*

Whenever a person is baptized into Christ they cross over from Spiritual Death to Spiritual Life, and they attain eternal life.

People love to assign labels to other people. They categorize people in ways that make sense to them. God, however, sees people in two fundamental states. They are either dead in their sins, or alive in Christ. Similarly, they are either in Christ, or not in Christ. They are either guilty of their sins, or forgiven of their sins. Look at these words from Jesus:

> *I told you that you would die in your sins; if you*
> *do not believe that I am he, you will indeed die*
> *in your sins." (John 8:24)*

One condition results in Spiritual Death, the other results in Spiritual Life.

Let's examine something that the apostle Paul has written, as follows:

> *As for you, you were dead in your transgressions*
> *and sins, in which you used to live when you*
> *followed the ways of this world and of the ruler*

of the kingdom of the air, the spirit who is now at work in those who are disobedient. All of us also lived among them at one time, gratifying the cravings of our flesh and following its desires and thoughts. Like the rest, we were by nature deserving of wrath. But because of his great love for us, God, who is rich in mercy, made us alive with Christ even when we were dead in transgressions—it is by grace you have been saved. (Ephesians 2:1-5)

In this passage, Paul is talking about the transition from Spiritual Death to Spiritual Life. He is pointing out that every person alive in Christ was once spiritually dead in their transgressions and sins. If a person is dead in transgressions and sins, then they are deserving of the wrath of God. The result of Spiritual Death is experiencing the wrath of God! Spiritual Death occurs when a person refuses to believe the truth about Jesus, and so be saved. Therefore, this means that people can be alive physically, but be spiritually dead to God at the same time.

The moment that Physical Death occurs, a person is cast into their eternal dwelling place. What people fail to realize is that although the body dies a Physical Death, all souls live forever. Therefore, people need to think beyond the physical and think spiritually. Jesus said a number of things that indicate this to be the case, consider for example:

"I tell you, my friends, do not be afraid of those who kill the body and after that can do no more. But I will show you whom you should fear: Fear him who, after your body has been killed, has

> **authority to throw you into hell. Yes, I tell you,**
> **fear him. (Luke 12:4-5)**

In Luke 16, Jesus gives the account of "The Rich Man and Lazarus." In this account, Jesus tells about what happens to people when they die their physical death. Those who are spiritually alive (right with God, or right in the sight of God) go immediately to the place of Paradise, escorted by angels. I am really looking forward to this part! Those who are spiritually dead go immediately to a place of torment. Without Christ there is no hope of eternal life with God. Without Christ there is only the promise of Physical Death accompanied by Spiritual Death. Without Christ a person is spiritually dead, and they will experience torment for eternity! The Bible speaks of hell, and eternal punishment frequently!

In my lifetime and in my ministry work, I have heard many people make jokes about the existence of hell. I have felt sorry for them, and I have prayed for many of them. They don't have a clue about what they are saying. They don't understand that hell is a very real place, and people really do go there. In addition, I have heard many people say that life in this world is hell. Likewise, they do not know what they are saying, and they are very confused. You should refrain from making jokes about heaven or hell. God is not pleased with such coarse joking.

> **Nor should there be obscenity, foolish talk or**
> **coarse joking, which are out of place, but rather**
> **thanksgiving. (Ephesians 5:4)**

Remember the words of Christ, and learn from Him daily. Don't ever believe anything from anyone, if what they say in any particular case conflicts with the words or teachings of Jesus and the Bible.

Other writings of Paul also provide great insight into the reality of eternal life. Paul knew that he was a servant of Christ, a bondservant to be exact, that he was right with God and that he was forgiven of his sins. He was a great proclaimer of the gospel and he is credited with writing at least 13 books of the New Testament. In his letter to the churches in Philippi, known as Philippians, he said the following:

> *If I am to go on living in the body, this will mean fruitful labor for me. Yet what shall I choose? I do not know! I am torn between the two: I desire to depart and be with Christ, which is better by far; ... (Philippians 1:22-23)*

Here Paul is indicating that he would rather depart from living in his physical body, and go to be in the presence of the Lord. That would be in the place of paradise! Remember that while on the cross Jesus said to one of the thieves next to Him, from Luke 23:43, **"Truly I tell you, today you will be with me in paradise."**

Finally, consider the words that Jesus spoke to his disciples to comfort them, as He knew He was approaching His time on the cross:

> *"Do not let your hearts be troubled. You believe in God; believe also in me. My Father's house has many rooms; if that were not so, would I have told you that I am going there to prepare a*

15

> *place for you? And if I go and prepare a place for*
> *you, I will come back and take you to be with me*
> *that you also may be where I am. (John 14:1-3)*

Therefore, every Christian can be assured that Jesus is preparing a place for them in His Father's house. If you are a Christian, you have an eternal dwelling place with the Lord! Know it. Believe it. Look forward to it.

Therefore, I plead with all people everywhere to get right with God, in Christ, and gain the assurance of eternal life while it is possible to do so! Today is the day of salvation! Do not be deceived, it's not good people that go to heaven. No one can be good enough on their own, apart from Jesus. No person can live a holy life, in the sight of God, apart from Christ and without the Holy Spirit of God within them. Rather, it is forgiven people that go to heaven! Therefore, get right with God in Christ and then remember this:

> *Since, then, you have been raised with Christ,*
> *set your hearts on things above, where Christ is,*
> *seated at the right hand of God. Set your minds*
> *on things above, not on earthly things. For you*
> *died, and your life is now hidden with Christ in*
> *God. When Christ, who is your life, appears,*
> *then you also will appear with him in glory.*
> *(Colossians 3:1-4)*

I want you to know that even though I am facing the end of my life in this world (my Physical Death), and my body is breaking down, I am not afraid.

> *Therefore we do not lose heart. Though outwardly we are wasting away, yet inwardly we are being renewed day by day. For our light and momentary troubles are achieving for us an eternal glory that far outweighs them all. So we fix our eyes not on what is seen, but on what is unseen, since what is seen is temporary, but what is unseen is eternal. (2 Corinthians 4:16-18)*

This passage has been my mantra since being diagnosed with cancer in January 2017. I have committed these verses, and many others, to memory and placed them in my heart. I encourage you to begin to memorize Bible verses, as soon as possible. They will be a daily source of strength and encouragement, as they keep you focused on the things of God.

I know that I have crossed over from death to life. I know and I have the assurance from Jesus that I will live, even though I may die. I have the confidence that comes from knowing. I have the strength that comes from Christ. (Philippians 4:13)

I am trusting in, relying on and placing myself in the hands of the Lord daily. That is the best place to be! I hope that you will do the same thing!

Understanding Salvation

Salvation is the most important thing that any person can learn about. Why? Well, because it has eternal implications. Too many people live their lives with a focus on earthly issues. In doing so, they neglect to consider their existence beyond and/or after the here and now. This is sad, and short-sighted. I want you to have a good foundation on the issue of salvation. I want you to be able to see the value that God places on salvation, as it is only possible due to the death of His Son. I want you to come to an understanding in your own mind that salvation is essential. That you must attain it. That without it you will be lost, and condemned to an eternity of punishment and torment in the place God calls hell. Pretty intense, right? I know. It is supposed to be. That's another thing. In our culture these days, no one talks much about the realities of going to hell. You need to be aware that every person, at some point, will either go to heaven or hell. I hope that you choose heaven. By the way, heaven and hell are the only two eternal options. Notice that I am using the terms of heaven and paradise interchangeably within this book. In addition, once God deems your eternal dwelling place it cannot and will not be changed. Therefore, learn all you can about the issue of salvation so you know where you will spend eternity.

The issue of salvation, which is being saved by the grace of God, is the most important aspect of Christianity. Salvation is the essence of the Christian faith. It is what compelled each and every person who is a Christian to become a Christian. It is having the assurance of salvation, that provides inner peace. By the way, most people desire inner peace. They may not know it, but deep within their hearts; they truly desire inner peace. Salvation provides the inner peace that people yearn to have, which cannot be provided by the world.

Salvation is something to be treasured. Something to be honored. Something to be thankful for on a continuous basis. Why? Because salvation is a gift from God.

> *For it is by grace you have been saved, through faith—and this is not from yourselves, it is the gift of God—not by works, so that no one can boast. (Ephesians 2:8-9)*

> *For the grace of God has appeared that offers salvation to all people. (Titus 2:11)*

Salvation provides inner peace because it means that a person no longer has to fear condemnation, being cast into hell, going to the place of torment, experiencing eternal damnation and being cast out into darkness away from the presence of the Lord and a myriad of other things. Once a person has salvation in and through Jesus they have peace. A peace that transcends logic. A peace that is present no matter what happens in the course of life. The apostle Paul knew this peace. The apostle Paul was moved by the Holy Spirit to write about this peace. Paul wrote:

> *Rejoice in the Lord always. I will say it again: Rejoice! Let your gentleness be evident to all. The Lord is near. Do not be anxious about anything,*

> *but in every situation, by prayer and petition,*
> *with thanksgiving, present your requests to God.*
> *And the peace of God, which transcends all*
> *understanding, will guard your hearts and your*
> *minds in Christ Jesus. (Philippians 4:4-7)*

As I undergo physical pain and the changes in my body, due to the cancer which is taking over my body, I want you to know that I have inner peace. Not only do I have peace, but the peace within me continues to increase. I am confident of my salvation. I know that I am right with God, in Christ. I know that while my body decays, my spirit grows. I am confident that I will continue to be at peace. I understand that life here in this world is temporary, but my life in Christ is eternal. Therefore, while my body decays I continue to focus on where I am going, and the fact that I will be in the presence of the Lord when I leave this world.

The peace that I have now, in the face of terminal illness, transcends my understanding. I don't know how it works. I can't explain it. I just know that I have it, praise God! I do, however, believe that if this diagnosis was given me before I became a Christian; that I would not have this same peace. It is a peace that comes from the Lord Jesus. I know this because Jesus said it was so. Here is what Jesus said regarding peace:

> *Peace I leave with you; my peace I give you. I*
> *do not give to you as the world gives. Do not*
> *let your hearts be troubled and do not be afraid.*
> *(John 14:27)*

Therefore, I urge you to stop seeking peace from the world, from worldly people and from worldly things. They cannot and will not be able to provide the peace that you seek. True peace, lasting peace and never-ending peace comes only from Jesus, when we are saved by Him and made right with God in Him. And, understand that peace displaces fear! People who live in a continual state of fear do not have peace. But once you are in Christ, everything changes. Once you are in Christ you have assurance. Once you are in Christ, there is nothing to fear.

> *Therefore, there is now no condemnation for those who are in Christ Jesus, because through Christ Jesus the law of the Spirit who gives life has set you free from the law of sin and death. (Romans 8:1-2)*
>
> *There is no fear in love. But perfect love drives out fear, because fear has to do with punishment. (1 John 4:18)*

Therefore, salvation provides the assurance of the things to come, when life in this world is over. It is the thing that mankind has been seeking since being created, and sin entered the world. It is having the assurance of an eternal life in the paradise of God. It is having the understanding that because you have put your hope in the work that Jesus did while on the cross, that you have been forgiven of your sins. It is knowing that Jesus did for you, what you could not do for yourself. In Christ, and Christ alone, you have been made righteous in the sight of God; and therefore, you have pledged your loyalty to the person of Jesus. It is knowing that by the name of Jesus you have been saved:

> *Jesus is "'the stone you builders rejected, which has become the cornerstone.' Salvation is found in no one else, for there is no other name under heaven given to mankind by which we must be saved." (Acts 4:11-12)*

Understanding salvation is relying on what Jesus has done for you, not on what you do for yourself, in order to be right with God. It is acknowledging that without the sacrificial act of Jesus, that you would be guilty of sins – deserving to be condemned.

It is knowing that apart from Christ you wouldn't stand a chance of being righteous – this is why the Scriptures say:

> *...for all have sinned and fall short of the glory of God, ... (Romans 3:23)*

Salvation is understanding that you have come to a point in your life when you realize that you need Jesus as your personal Savior. That Jesus is the Savior of the world. That without Jesus you would be found guilty of your sins, and condemned to eternal punishment (Spiritual Death).

This is why the Scriptures say:

> *For the wages of sin is death, but the gift of God is eternal life in Christ Jesus our Lord. (Romans 6:23)*

There is something else that you need to remember about salvation. When you were saved, you became a child of the one true living God. God is now your Father. Always remember this. And, keep in mind that He is a perfect Father. He never makes mistakes. He never makes a bad decision. He never disciplines you with impure intent. Your heavenly Father is always there for you. He always cares for you. He always loves you. He is always helping you. He is always working for you. Everything that He allows to happen to you; and everything that He allows you to experience is meant for your good.

> *And we know that in all things God works for the good of those who love him, who have been called according to his purpose. (Romans 8:28)*

If you are not yet assured of your salvation, then please do whatever it takes for you to gain that assurance. Please realize, however, that salvation is NOT based upon the following factors:

- The kind of life you live
- How nice you are to people
- Doing more good things than bad things in your life
- How much money you give to charity
- How you grew up
- Your view of how God should operate with regard to your eternal dwelling place

It should be clear to you, but just in case it isn't; be advised that you cannot do anything on your own apart from Jesus that will result in you being saved. Salvation is a free gift offering from God. God has provided Jesus so that everyone could be saved, and not suffer the due penalty of their sins.

> *For there is one God and one mediator between God and mankind, the man Christ Jesus, who gave himself as a ransom for all people. (1 Timothy 2:5-6)*

Jesus willingly went to the cross. Yes, that's right, Jesus went to the cross on his own accord. The Jews didn't put Him there. The Romans didn't put him there. We all put Him there. He went on his own free will, in accordance with the will of His Father to save all who put their trust in Him. And it wasn't easy. It was a struggle! In this regard, Jesus provides us with a great example of how to respond when we are facing tough times. Jesus wanted the will of His Father to be done, over His own will. Consider the fact that Jesus said this just before going to the cross:

> *"Father, if you are willing, take this cup from me; yet not my will, but yours be done." (Luke 22:42)*

There is a lot of confusion in the world today regarding the issue of salvation, and going to heaven. This is sad. Unfortunately, people believe that their conviction about an issue guarantees their accuracy on an issue. It doesn't! Many people have been sincerely convicted on a particular issue or subject, and have been sincerely wrong. Don't become one of them. Such people create their own theology, basing the outcomes of things in their favor. This is a bad move. The only one who gets to decide anything on such issues is God. Make sure, therefore, that you listen to Him. Make sure you do things God's way. Make sure you have heard from Him on all issues and subjects, before you make a decision about what you believe, and why you believe it. In this book I have tried to lay things out, as well as possible, in order for anyone to learn from my discoveries, mistakes and understandings of God. I have done so out of my love for people everywhere. Even still, I don't expect anyone to accept what I say without questioning, without seeking and without looking into the Word of God for God's answers and guidance.

In summary, however, remember that in order to be saved you must know Jesus (the Christ) as your Lord and Savior. In order to be saved, you must be united in the death, burial and resurrection of Christ. In order to be saved, you must trust in the blood of Christ to cleanse you of your sins. Being saved is the most amazing thing that can ever happen to you. Please maintain your sense of awe on this matter. Remembering what God has done for you in and through Christ will keep you thankful. It will also keep you humble, and it will help propel you to share "The Good News" with other people. Once saved, however, don't use your salvation as a means to continue to sin. Don't sin because you know that you have the grace of God "in your favor," or "on your side." Therefore, always remember as a Christian:

> *You, my brothers and sisters, were called to be free. But do not use your freedom to indulge the flesh; rather serve one another humbly in love. (Galatians 5:13)*

Finally, I want you to know that having a relationship with God, in and through Christ, is not complicated. God, in His desire to have people reconciled to Himself, made His plan of salvation quite simple. Sadly, however, for all kinds of ungodly reasons; man has complicated the entire notion of salvation. Some have made it more complicated, than what God has said. Others have made it easier. Therefore, I am pleading with you to go by-the-book. Ok, I'll say it clearly, go by the Bible. If you do, you won't go wrong!

Sin, Forgiveness and Becoming a Christian

Y ou need to understand that your life, future and every relationship you will ever have depends on and hinges on your closeness to God, and His forgiveness. Once you have sinned, if you are old enough to know better, your relationship with God has been severed. At some point when you reach a certain age and/or understanding, God will hold you accountable for your sins. This is often referred to as the age of accountability, and it is determined by God as He knows your mind and heart. Therefore, when you have reached the age or mental capacity of accountability and you sin; in that moment of time, your relationship with God has been severed. In addition, please understand and remember that sin takes many forms. There are sins of omission as well as sins of commission.

Sins of omission are the things that we know we should be doing, which are good, but we refuse to do.

If anyone, then, knows the good they ought to do and doesn't do it, it is sin for them. (James 4:17)

Sins of commission are the things that we shouldn't be doing, which are displeasing in the eyes of God, that we do. And, of course, sin can also occur in the heart. Whatever the case, sins that we are held accountable for separate us from God.

> *Surely the arm of the LORD is not too short to*
> *save, nor his ear too dull to hear.*
> *But your iniquities have separated you from*
> *your God;*
> *your sins have hidden his face from you,*
> *so that he will not hear. (Isaiah 59:1-2)*

By the time you are able to read and understand these things, it is very likely that you are at the age of being accountable. It is paramount that you realize this. But don't be disheartened, as God has provided a way for you to be reconciled to Him. The way back to God, and the way to be forgiven of your sins is in the person of Jesus. Jesus said,

> *I am the way and the truth and the life. No one*
> *comes to the Father except through me. (John*
> *14:6)*

You must understand that you have sinned, and as a result of your sin, your relationship with God has been lost. Furthermore, you must desire to be forgiven by God by being washed by the blood of Christ. Jesus is the lamb of God who takes away the sin of the world. (John 1)

Your lost relationship with God is restored and/or reconciled, after you have heard the gospel (The Good News) of Jesus. After you believe that the gospel of Jesus is true. After you confess Jesus as Lord, and most importantly after you are baptized into Jesus for the forgiveness of your sins. At that time, you will be forgiven by God and receive His Holy Spirit. Consider this passage:

> *"Therefore let all Israel be assured of this: God has made this Jesus, whom you crucified, both Lord and Messiah." When the people heard this, they were cut to the heart and said to Peter and the other apostles, "Brothers, what shall we do?"*
> *Peter replied, "Repent and be baptized, every one of you, in the name of Jesus Christ for the forgiveness of your sins. And you will receive the gift of the Holy Spirit. The promise is for you and your children and for all who are far off—for all whom the Lord our God will call." With many other words he warned them; and he pleaded with them, "Save yourselves from this corrupt generation." (Acts 2:36-40).*

God has given a promise here, and God honors His promises! Furthermore, God has not done anything to nullify this promise. So, once you have been baptized into Jesus, the Christ, you are forgiven by God. All of your sins; past, present and future will be and have been washed away by the blood of Jesus. That means that God will never hold any of your sins against you. That's right NEVER! It's just as if your sins never happened. That's one of the ways that I like to think about justification. You must, however, maintain your relationship with God in and through Christ. You must continue to walk in the light of Christ.

> *But if we walk in the light, as he is in the light, we have fellowship with one another, and the blood of Jesus, his Son, purifies us from all sin. (1 John 1:7)*

Treasure this forgiveness! Don't take it for granted, and always be thankful for the gift that God provided to you in His Son.

> *For God so loved the world that he gave his one and only Son, that whoever believes in him shall not perish but have eternal life. (John 3:16)*

There may be people that say that you don't need to be baptized to be saved, or forgiven. Don't believe them. But, don't feel that you have to argue with them. You don't. Try to remember that anyone who listens to Jesus is on the side of truth. Anyone who promotes the cause and the case of Christ is moving in the direction of the Kingdom of Heaven and God, which is a good thing. Just make sure you continue to move in that direction, and end up entering the Kingdom of God yourself. So, instead of listening to people, listen to what the Scriptures say. The Scriptures are the "Word of God." (2 Timothy 3:16-17)

I will address this more for you in a later chapter. However, for now, here is a quote from Jesus on the importance of baptism:

He (Jesus) said to them (His disciples),

> *"Go into all the world and preach the gospel to all creation. Whoever believes and is baptized will be saved, but whoever does not believe will be condemned. (Mark 16:15-16)*

The moment you are baptized into Christ a number of things happen, as follows:

- You Are Forgiven of Your Sins

- You Are Born Again by The Power of God's Holy Spirit
- You Are a Child of The One True Living God
- You Are Added as a Member to the Lord's Church, the body of Christ – By Christ
- You Become a Christian
- You have the Assurance of Salvation
- YOU CAN LOOK FORWARD TO GOING TO HEAVEN WHEN LEAVING THIS WORLD

While I can't and wouldn't, even if I could, force you to become a Christian; it is the path I would choose for you. I hope that this is the path that you will choose for yourself. Please give Jesus a chance. I want you to know that there is no one else anywhere at any time who will love you, care for you and take care of you as Jesus will.

There is another component that pertains to forgiveness. You must forgive other people of their sins. That is what God demands of you. Jesus said that if we want to be forgiven by God, then we must forgive other people:

> *For if you forgive other people when they sin against you, your heavenly Father will also forgive you. But if you do not forgive others their sins, your Father will not forgive your sins. (Matthew 6:14-15)*

This forgiveness should not be something that you feel that you are forced to do. Rather, desire to forgive people. Make it a priority in your life, mind and heart. The forgiveness that you offer to other people will be like salve to your soul. It will be good for you, it will be refreshing for you. It will help you to be free to be all that God wants you to be.

Unforgiveness, on the other hand, is like poison to your soul. Unforgiveness will eat at you from the inside-out. It will damage your soul. I will impede your growth. Understand that unforgiveness will make you miserable.

One more thing, don't hold forgiveness back from people because they didn't ask for it. That is not what God desires. Learn to and desire to forgive people, whether they ask for your forgiveness or not. When Jesus was on the cross being crucified, He asked His Father to forgive them.

> *"Father, forgive them, for they do not know what they are doing." (Luke 23:34)*

Desire to and learn to forgive as God forgives!

Before I close on this topic, there is one more issue I feel compelled to discuss. I believe that the church's view of itself and the world has been misunderstood. Therefore, as you are a member of the body of Christ, I implore you to reconcile this misunderstanding. Help people to realize that Christians don't think that they are better than non-Christians. Help people to understand that Christians don't hate non-Christians. Help people to understand that the difference between a Christian and a non-Christian is the issue of being forgiven of sin, and being right in the sight of God. This, however, has nothing to do with the qualities of any individual. Rather, it has to do with the love of the Father, and the obedience of His Son Jesus – the Christ. Because of this, and so many other reasons, no person should boast about their position with God in Christ. Paul stated this beautifully in the Scriptures:

> *It is because of him that you are in Christ Jesus, who has become for us wisdom from God—that is, our righteousness, holiness and redemption. Therefore, as it is written: "Let the one who boasts boast in the Lord." (1 Corinthians 1:30-31)*

Live to help the unforgiven become forgiven in Christ Jesus. Live to spread the message of the gospel. Live to help people understand what Christianity is truly about.

And, most of all, remember this. The focus of Christianity isn't about a set of rules. It isn't about dos and don'ts. No, far from it! The essence of Christianity is about relationship. It is about being in a right relationship with God, in and through Christ.

The Essence of Love

L ove is the most important attribute that any person can possess. It is a quality that we see in God, and experience from God. So, it is by knowing and learning from God that we learn the truth about love. God, out of His love, gave His Son Jesus in order for mankind to be reconciled with Him, and have eternal life.

> *For God so loved the world that he gave his one and only Son, that whoever believes in him shall not perish but have eternal life. (John 3:16)*

Most people, however, don't understand the meaning of love. Much of the time there is confusion on this subject. The only way to understand the essence of love is to be loved by God, and love God in return. As a young man I thought I knew a lot about love. I was so wrong. I didn't have a clue about love. Actually, what I did know about was lust. Oh yeah, I knew a lot about lust. This is true for many people. Lust is often confused with and displaces love. It is crucial for you to know the difference, so that you don't make a big mistake and cause yourself pain and suffering. Lust leads to sin, and sin leads to pain and suffering. Lust, not love, for example; can be what drives people to have one marriage or relationship after another. In such situations people are actually lusting after a specific person. Then, once that lust has been satisfied (or even if it hasn't) the relationship and/or the marriage is over. They often develop lustful feelings and desires for another person, and the cycle begins again. Until that person learns about love, they will continue in this pattern. Remember and always be mindful of the damage that lust can cause. Lust has destroyed many marriages.

God's Word is packed full of information on the essence of love. If you want to know what love is, you must learn about it from God. Read His Word. Study His Word. Live-out His Word, and you will understand and experience the essence of love!

Love is more than having a specific feeling or emotion. Think about how you feel when you see a really cute puppy. There is an emotion stirred within you, and you develop a desire to possess the puppy. What are you thinking about in that moment? Well, most likely, you will probably be thinking about how nice it would be to have that puppy around to make you feel the way you feel right now. In this case, you are thinking about yourself. You are focused on your feelings, and how having the puppy will benefit you. Are you thinking about taking care of the puppy? Are you thinking about providing the puppy with food, shelter and medical care? Are you thinking about how you can provide the puppy with a good home and a pleasant life? Maybe, maybe not. The point here is that love is actually taking action to benefit someone else. In this case, thinking about and taking action to benefit the puppy is loving the puppy. Anything short of this is merely lusting after the puppy, and desiring to have it as a prized possession. Thinking of another person as a prized possession is a result of lust, not love. Such thoughts center on self, and help us to see the difference between lust and love. Again, we see love and lust differentiated and defined for us in the Bible. Again, we see the essence of love demonstrated for us by what God has done for us.

> *But God demonstrates his own love for us in this: While we were still sinners, Christ died for us. (Romans 5:8)*

> *This is love: not that we loved God, but that he loved us and sent his Son as an atoning sacrifice for our sins. (1 John 4:10)*

There are many things that you need to and should understand about love. First and foremost, always remember that the essence of God is love. God loves all people, of course, but more than that; God is love.

> *Whoever does not love does not know God, because God is love. (1 John 4:8)*

> *And so we know and rely on the love God has for us. God is love. Whoever lives in love lives in God, and God in them. (1 John 4:16)*

One of the best-known chapters of the Bible is 1 Corinthians 13. This chapter provides a most excellent description of love. I have performed many wedding ceremonies in my time as a minister, and parts of this chapter have been included in each ceremony that I performed. I want you to see the words that God uses to describe love. So, take a look:

If I speak in the tongues of men or of angels, but do not have love, I am only a resounding gong or a clanging cymbal. If I have the gift of prophecy and can fathom all mysteries and all knowledge, and if I have a faith that can move mountains, but do not have love, I am nothing. If I give all I possess to the poor and give over my body to hardship that I may boast, but do not have love, I gain nothing.

Love is patient, love is kind. It does not envy, it does not boast, it is not proud. It does not dishonor others, it is not self-seeking, it is not easily angered, it keeps no record of wrongs.

Love does not delight in evil but rejoices with the truth.

It always protects, always trusts, always hopes, always perseveres.

Love never fails. But where there are prophecies, they will cease; where there are tongues, they will be stilled; where there is knowledge, it will pass away. For we know in part and we prophesy in part, but when completeness comes, what is in part disappears. When I was a child, I talked like a child, I thought like a child, I reasoned like a child. When I became a man, I put the ways of childhood behind me. For now we see only a reflection as in a mirror; then we shall see face to face. Now I know in part; then I shall know fully, even as I am fully known.

And now these three remain: faith, hope and love. But the greatest of these is love. (1 Corinthians 13:1-13)

God has provided us with this beautiful passage of Scripture to understand His love for us, and how we are supposed to love others. In this passage, the apostle Paul is noting that all that we do, even if it is good, is meaningless without love. The type of love described here is known as "Agape" love. This is the essence of the love God has shown all human kind. Agape love is a sacrificial love. Agape love is a pre-determined love. Agape love is a deliberate love, which is not contingent on the response of the person receiving the love shown. It is often referred to as "unconditional love."

Therefore, always remember that God's love for you is NOT based on your performance. On the contrary, God's love for you is based on the fact that you are one of His magnificent creations! God loves you more than you can understand or imagine right now! He loves me more than I can understand or imagine right now. However, I believe that soon and very soon; I will have a complete understanding of His love for me. When I leave this world, and enter into the presence of the Lord in His Heavenly Kingdom, it will become crystal clear! The entire notion of love based on performance is a worldly concept. Please learn to disregard worldly views and opinions when considering the things of God. God's ways are higher than our ways. God's thoughts are higher than our thoughts! (Isaiah 55:9)

And, when you make mistakes don't lose heart, and do not let your heart be troubled. Remember that God loves you even when you make a mistake. He loves you even when you sin. Yes, of course, God is disappointed in you when you sin; but He still loves you even when you sin. He loves you even when you behave in ways that are not fitting for a Christian. When Peter denied knowing Jesus, three times, Jesus didn't stop loving him. When all the disciples let Him down, Jesus did not stop loving them. Well, maybe Judas was an exception!

> *While I (Jesus) was with them, I protected them (the disciples) and kept them safe by that name you gave me. None has been lost except the one doomed to destruction so that Scripture would be fulfilled. (John 17:12)*

The love that Jesus has for you is deeper, wider and greater than you know! Take comfort in knowing these things, and treasure the love God has for you in your heart. Also, remember that discipline accompanies sin. Your heavenly Father loves you, so He will discipline you when you do wrong! Let's look at some passages from Hebrews that support this.

> *"My son, do not make light of the Lord's discipline, and do not lose heart when he rebukes you, because the Lord disciplines the one he loves, and he chastens everyone he accepts as his son." (Hebrews 12:5-6)*

Loving earthly fathers discipline their children. They understand the value in discipline. If they do this, with good intention, how much more will your heavenly Father discipline you?

It will be painful, but it will also be beneficial. Learn to accept it! Learn to be trained by it!

> *Moreover, we have all had human fathers who disciplined us and we respected them for it. How much more should we submit to the Father of spirits and live! They disciplined us for a little*

> *while as they thought best; but God disciplines us for our good, in order that we may share in his holiness. No discipline seems pleasant at the time, but painful. Later on, however, it produces a harvest of righteousness and peace for those who have been trained by it. (Hebrew 12:9-11)*

There is another thing I want to address for you in this chapter. I am addressing it here because it is somewhat linked to the essence of love. It is the matter of understanding your true value. The world may try to convince you that you are only valuable under certain conditions. Worldly people may try to tell you that your value is determined by how good looking you are, or by how much money you have acquired or the accomplishments you have achieved in work or play. Don't listen to them, and don't believe them! I want you to understand that you are extremely valuable to God. He created you, and His love for you is amazing. Therefore, I want you to be on-guard against low self-esteem. When other people attempt to diminish your value, remember that Jesus died for you. That speaks volumes on how much God values you. When you understand the value that God places on you, then you will be able to see the true value of others.

God gave His Son Jesus for all of mankind, and those who receive Him are blessed beyond measure. I hope that you receive and respond to the love God has offered to you in Christ. If you do, you will love God. If you do, you will become a follower of Christ. If you do, you will love Jesus. If you do, you will obey the commandments of Jesus and the Bible. If you do, you will live in accordance with the example of Jesus, and love as He loves.

Let me offer you one more Scripture reference on the essence of love:

> ***This is how we know what love is: Jesus Christ laid down his life for us. And we ought to lay down our lives for our brothers and sisters. (1 John 3:16)***

So, there you have it, this is the essence of love!

Living To Please God

Once again, using myself as the subject of study, I want to help you learn about a very important issue. The issue of coming to terms with regard to how you live your life. Before I became a Christian, I was all about living my life my way. I was the one that dictated what was good and what was bad for me. My way, at this time in my life, was the best way – at least that's what I thought. But I did not come to this conclusion on my own, ironically enough. The culture in America at the time, and I'm speaking of the mid 1970's, was undergoing a strong movement for and about self-actualization. In fact, the U. S. Army adopted a promotional campaign on the issue of self-actualization. The tag-line of the campaign was, "Be All You Can Be!" And by the way, you get to be the one that determines what you can be. I have grown increasingly convinced that the mid 1970s was a turning point for the youth of America. A turning point with regard to teaching our youth that they were the best ones to determine what was good for them. That they didn't really need to seek out counsel or guidance with regard to major decisions in life. Another aspect and proof of this movement was prevalent in the music that was being produced, during this same period. Frank Sinatra released a song in 1969 that was called, "My Way." This song presents a braggadocios point of view from a person who earned success in their chosen career field claiming with gladness that they did it "My Way." This song became a huge hit for Sinatra, as well as becoming a 70's classic. It is now 2017, and this song is still played in many venues and at many special events.

My mother loved the crooners. She played records by Frank Sinatra, Perry Como, Dean Martin and a host of others on a regular basis. Take some time and look these men up. Anyway, I can still remember hearing Frank's voice echoing in our house on Saturday mornings. My mom played records as she cleaned the house. Oh yeah, you may not understand what records are. Wow, I really sound like an old person now. She cranked up the volume so she could hear the music anywhere as she moved about the house. So, I had the words of this song ingrained into my head. And here's the point. There is a line in the song that says this, "The right to say the things he feels and not the words of one who kneels!" I didn't realize it at the time, but this line is actually speaking out against being a man of prayer. Ouch, that hurt! So, what I'm saying here is that I had some help developing the mind-set that I had. So, let that be part of the lesson. Remember that no matter how people try to influence you, no matter what people say to you, and no matter how many times they try to beat their beliefs into your brain; you are responsible for the views and opinions that you follow and express. Ultimately, you will be the one to suffer if you fail to understand this. Again, I offer this point of guidance and counsel. Always be aware of what you believe, and why you believe what you believe on any particular issue or subject.

Later on, after I had caused myself a lot of grief and aggravation, as I was studying the Bible; I came to a level of new understanding. It was an understanding that I should have been turning to God, and His Word, in order to determine what was best for me. It was an understanding that I should have been living to please God, rather than living to please myself.

And this made sense, after the fact. After all, shouldn't God know what's best for me? Shouldn't God know the best way for me to live my life? Of course, He should, He created me. He is my heavenly Father. He is the all-knowing eternal and infinite being!

The apostles understood this point. They understood that God alone had the best knowledge of what would be good for them. More than this, however, they understood that their lives no longer belonged to them. They understood and advised that they had the mandate, and the desire, to live their lives to please God. That they died to self. Let's focus in on some Scriptures that identify these points:

Here is what the apostle Paul had to say:

> *However, I consider my life worth nothing to me; my only aim is to finish the race and complete the task the Lord Jesus has given me—the task of testifying to the good news of God's grace. (Acts 20:24)*

Here we see Paul giving testimony that his life is no longer under his direction, and subject to his own desires. He once was an enemy of the gospel, and the church. He had set his mind on persecuting the followers of Christ, and killing them in the name of his god. But since becoming a Christian himself, things changed. As a devout Christian and evangelist, he would live to proclaim the gospel of Christ. He became committed to doing what Christ told him to do. He would now focus on doing good! Doing what was deemed good by God, and not as he understood it. Let this be a lesson for you as well. As a Christian, your life no longer belongs to you. If this is confusing to you, don't be overly concerned. However, continue to read and study the Scriptures. Things will become clear.

Let's also consider some additional writings of the apostle Paul.

> **Since, then, you have been raised with Christ, set your hearts on things above, where Christ is, seated at the right hand of God. Set your minds on things above, not on earthly things. For you died, and your life is now hidden with Christ in God. When Christ, who is your life, appears, then you also will appear with him in glory. (Colossians 3:1-4)**

As Paul continues to write, he provides very specific instructions regarding how a person must live since they have been made alive in Christ. Colossians Chapter 3 has been extremely helpful, and convicting, in my walk with and for the Lord. I hope it is that for you as well. I urge you to make a habit of reading this particular chapter on a regular basis.

The apostle Peter wrote two letters, which also include directions on living to please God. I urge you to read, study and adapt a way of life commensurate with these letters. Here is what Peter wrote as part of 1 Peter:

> *Therefore, since Christ suffered in his body, arm yourselves also with the same attitude, because whoever suffers in the body is done with sin. As a result, they do not live the rest of their earthly lives for evil human desires, but rather for the will of God. (1 Peter 4:1-2)*

Ok, well, here is the most important thing that you need to understand about living to please God. When you live your life to please yourself, or other people, you will be left feeling empty and void of meaningful purpose. Living without purpose is one of the worst things that can happen to a person. In my exposure to suicide and in my study of suicide prevention, with the Maryland State Police, I have come to realize that the loss of purpose is a major factor in why people are moved to commit suicide. God wants us to have a strong sense of purpose. When you live to please God and glorify Him every day, you have a meaningful purpose. With such purpose life is fruitful, exciting and worth living. Not only that, but you will experience a peace and joy that nothing else can provide. You will have the knowledge and understanding that you are doing what God wants you to do. So, stop measuring success and accomplishments in worldly ways. Start envisioning success as a life lived to please God!

Finally, I want you to understand that living to please God should be a desire that burns within you. It shouldn't be a cloud that hangs over your head. Something that you do because you have to do it. Not something that you do because you feel obligated, even though you are. No, it should be a desire you have because of the gratitude you have in your heart, mind and soul because of what God has done for you in Christ. It is your desire because you have been delivered from an empty way of life. Delivered from the life you once lived, when you were forgiven of your sins.

This entire concept has been captured and presented to us in Paul's letter to Titus:

> *Remind the people to be subject to rulers and authorities, to be obedient, to be ready to do whatever is good, to slander no one, to be peaceable and considerate, and always to be gentle toward everyone.*
> *At one time we too were foolish, disobedient, deceived and enslaved by all kinds of passions and pleasures. We lived in malice and envy, being hated and hating one another. But when the kindness and love of God our Savior appeared, he saved us, not because of righteous things we had done, but because of his mercy. He saved us through the washing of rebirth and renewal by the Holy Spirit, whom he poured out on us generously through Jesus Christ our Savior, so that, having been justified by his grace, we might become heirs having the hope of eternal life. This is a trustworthy saying. And I want you to stress these things, so that those who have trusted in God may be careful to devote themselves to doing what is good. These things are excellent and profitable for everyone. (Titus 3:1-8)*

Always remember that in becoming a Christian, you died to yourself. You have been crucified with Christ. Paul knew this:

> *I have been crucified with Christ and I no longer live, but Christ lives in me. The life I now live in the body, I live by faith in the Son of God, who loved me and gave himself for me. (Galatians 2:20)*

Paul's letter to the church in Ephesus (known as Ephesians) has always been very important to me, for many reasons. Along with the letters of Peter, and the book of James I have found Paul's letters to be very helpful in understanding how to live to please God. Ephesians has six chapters. I have seen that in Chapters 1-3 Paul outlines the blessings that all Christians have, because of getting right with God in Christ. However, in Chapters 4-6 Paul outlines the responsibilities that Christians have because of the blessings received. Study these chapters carefully, and find out what pleases the Lord!

Learning From Jesus and The Bible Daily

L earning is part of life. It is what helps to make life exciting and fun. It is part of your growth process. You should have a desire to learn, and you should be willing to share what you have learned to help and benefit other people. Learning helps to satisfy the soul, body and spirit.

That said, understand that there is no greater teacher than the Lord Jesus. He has things to teach you that you cannot learn from anyone else. He has things to teach you that are more important than the things you will learn from anyone else. So, I encourage you to learn from Jesus each and every day. How? By studying the life and the teachings of Jesus preserved for us in the four gospel accounts (Matthew, Mark, Luke and John). In these gospels you will not only learn from Jesus, but you will also learn about who He was. You will see how He lived. How He loved. How He shared with other people. In these gospels God allows us to see the life of Christ. The life that was lived in total obedience to the Father, and was sacrificed so that you and I could have eternal life. In these gospels, you will also be introduced to the men that really knew Him. You will learn about the choices that they made pertaining to Jesus, and the sacrifices that they made to be His disciples (a disciple is a student or learner of). In these gospels you will come to understand what it means to be a true disciple, and the benefits that you will reap from being a disciple. Here is one of the things that Jesus said about discipleship:

> *"If you hold to my teaching, you are really my disciples. Then you will know the truth, and the truth will set you free." (John 8:31-32)*

Here is another thing that Jesus said about being a disciple:

> *"Whoever wants to be my disciple must deny themselves and take up their cross and follow me. For whoever wants to save their life will lose it, but whoever loses their life for me will find it. (Matthew 16:24-25)*

I have written another section titled, "Living To Please God." You are called to live to please God, no doubt, and learning from Jesus will enable you to do so. By embracing the teachings of Jesus, and studying the Bible daily, you will be equipped with the knowledge and understanding needed to live a life pleasing to God. Not only that, but remember as a Christian you have the Holy Spirit of God within you. With the Word of God and the Spirit of God you have the ability to live for God, and to please Him.

As I was growing up, I did not have anyone in my life that was a devout believer in Jesus or the Bible. In fact, just the opposite. I grew up with a disbelief in Jesus as the Son of God. I grew up in the Jewish Faith. In the course of my learning, in this faith, my focus was directed to the Old Testament. The Jewish Bible, also known as the Tanakh, is comprised only of the books of the Old Testament. Nothing of the New Testament, as you should study, was included in the Tanakh. Anyway, this left a huge void in my understanding of many things. I did celebrate my Bar-Mitzvah when I was thirteen years old, as the tradition of the faith prompted. However, after that I became more about life than religion. Sadly, much of what I learned about many important topics was learned from worldly people. My mind and my character were shaped by worldly points of view. Please do not let this happen to you. This would be a tragedy. It is to avoid such a tragedy that I am writing this book for you.

By the way, today is Saturday December 16, 2017. The last few days have been fairly significant for me health wise. I have developed edema (fluid build-up) in my abdomen, arms, legs and chest. Marti has been on the phone early this morning with our palliative/ hospice care provider, and other medical professionals. I will likely be transitioning from palliative care to hospice care sometime next week. People are put into hospice care when a medical professional certifies that, in their best opinion, the person has less than six-months to live. The reason that I am saying this is very important, and applicable to learning from Jesus and the Bible daily. Because of what I have learned and what I have done, I am now prepared to face the transition from life in this body to going to be with the Lord in Paradise. I would not be prepared had I never listened to and obeyed the teachings of Jesus. Remember, knowing is one thing; doing is quite another!

Before I became a Christian, I had a worldly mindset. From the 1951 movie, "The Christmas Carol," which is one of my favorite movies; "I was a man with a worldly mind." I focused on many of the wrong things. I listened to worldly people, and I participated in worldly activities. It wasn't until I began reading the Bible and learning from Jesus that I understood and realized how messed-up I was. I realized that I had to change my way of thinking in a major way. I had to unlearn and let go of all the worldly teachings I had accepted, and grasp the teachings of all things God revealed in the life of Christ and the Bible. As I learned from Jesus, I began to see things in an entirely new way. I began to see things from a godly perspective, not from a worldly perspective, and I also began to understand why such things were important. In essence, I was undergoing a transformation. I was being transformed by a renewing of my mind. This is noted in one of Paul's letters known as Romans:

> *Do not conform to the pattern of this world, but be transformed by the renewing of your mind. Then you will be able to test and approve what God's will is—his good, pleasing and perfect will. (Romans 12:2)*

Before Jesus was crucified, while standing before Pilate, he said:

> *In fact, the reason I was born and came into the world is to testify to the truth. Everyone on the side of truth listens to me." (John 18:37)*

As I was being transformed by the renewing of my mind I realized, in spite of all the sin in my life and in spite of all the corrupt thinking I had done in the past; I did have a yearning for the truth. As a result, I was moved to listen to Jesus. I have been trying to learn from Jesus and the Bible every day of my life, since I started seeking Him in the Summer of 1993. Ironically, my journey with Jesus began when my sister Elise, who was 5 years older than me, was diagnosed with terminal lung cancer. That was the first time in my life that I felt a real need for Jesus.

I am pleading with you to seek out, to find and to learn from Jesus and the Bible before there is a crisis in your life. If you do, you will be better prepared for anything that comes at you. Learn, grow and thrive by learning from the one who created you and sustains you each and every day of your life. Yes, learn from Jesus daily. That is the best advice I can give you. So, then, I urge you to carve out for yourself a certain amount of time each day in which you read and study the Bible. Initially, don't focus too much on the time spent doing it. Rather, focus on developing the habit. Once you make it a habit, you can always increase the time. The time you spend reading and studying the Bible is priceless!

Spiritual Warfare

I need to tell you some things. Some things that may seem very scary to you. It would hurt my heart, deeply, to know that I scared you. However, it is worth the risk. You need to have this information. You need to be made aware of these things. So, it is with your benefit in mind that I write these things for you here and now. I could write a lot on this issue. However, since I am intending to inform you without frightening you; I will merely address some key points on which you can build upon at your own speed and at your own pace. So, here it is. I want you to know that you are in a fight. It is a fight of good vs. evil. A fight of God vs. Satan. A fight of salvation vs. damnation. And, even though you can't see them; there are angels all around you right now! They are fighting for you.

Whether you believe it or not, whether you accept it or not and whether you like it or not; it's a fact! There is a fight being waged by the enemy of God, Satan, over your soul. Not only that, but Satan is waging a war against God for the soul of every person that is alive. Satan is looking for any way he can to steal a person away from God and keep them from gaining salvation in and through Jesus. Jesus alluded to this, and John has recorded it for us:

> *The thief (Satan) comes only to steal and kill and destroy; I (Jesus) have come that they may have life, and have it to the full. (John 10:10)*

Satan wants to steal the souls of people. If he is able to do this, then they are taken captive to do his will. Satan takes people captive to do his will, when they oppose the gospel of Jesus. This is clearly noted for us. In fact, when this happens people may not even be aware that it has happened.

> *Opponents (people who oppose the gospel message) must be gently instructed, in the hope that God will grant them repentance leading them to a knowledge of the truth, and that they will come to their senses and escape from the trap of the devil, who has taken them captive to do his will. (2 Timothy 2:25-26)*

Satan also uses his power and influence to keep people from seeing Jesus as the Savior. Paul put it like this:

> *The god of this age (Satan) has blinded the minds of unbelievers, so that they cannot see the light of the gospel that displays the glory of Christ, who is the image of God. (2 Corinthians 4:4)*

Satan does this because he desires to kill people before they get right with God. If he is able to do this, then he has gained their soul and they are his for eternity. Why does Satan want to do this? Well, one reason is because he is angry with God and wants to hurt God. Satan wanted to be like God, rather than worship God. As a result, Satan lost his place in heaven. God does not tolerate any one who wants to take His place. Remember that, and realize that some people are still trying to do this very thing. Anyway, Satan uses his power against people. Since Satan is no match for God, and he can't go up against God directly, he wants to and sets out to hurt people. Satan knows that when people get hurt by him, it really hurts God.

Satan also seeks to devour the children of God in and through sin. Peter wrote about this, and provided a warning on this to all Christians:

> *Be alert and of sober mind. Your enemy the devil prowls around like a roaring lion looking for someone to devour. (1 Peter 5:8)*

Make sure that you, even as a follower of Christ, are not executing the will of Satan. Oh, yes, it can happen. There was a time when Jesus was talking to Peter. Jesus told Peter what was going to happen. Jesus was predicting His own death. Well, Peter wanted to stop that from happening. Here is what happened:

> *Jesus turned and said to Peter, "Get behind me, Satan! You are a stumbling block to me; you do not have in mind the concerns of God, but merely human concerns." (Matthew 16:23)*

Satan is working hard and uses the tactics of spiritual warfare to achieve his objectives.

For instance, Satan will use lies, half-truths, sin and the desires of the flesh to steal your soul away. Look at what Peter wrote:

> *Dear friends, I urge you, as foreigners and exiles, to abstain from sinful desires, which wage war against your soul. (1 Peter 2:11)*

Therefore, considering all of this information, make sure that you get on, and stay on the side of truth – which is the side of God the Father, God the Son and God the Holy Spirit.

Once you are right with God, rely on the power of the Lord in this spiritual battle. For the Lord has and will give you everything you need to have victory. Paul wrote this to the church in Ephesus:

> *Finally, be strong in the Lord and in his mighty power. Put on the full armor of God, so that you can take your stand against the devil's schemes. For our struggle is not against flesh and blood, but against the rulers, against the authorities, against the powers of this dark world and against the spiritual forces of evil in the heavenly realms. Therefore put on the full armor of God, so that when the day of evil comes, you may be able to stand your ground, and after you have done everything, to stand. (Ephesians 6:10-13)*

There is another point that I want to make here, even though it may be a bit difficult to understand, regarding when people hurt you. When they say terrible things to you. When they lie about you. Whenever they commit any kind of evil against you, they are doing so because they are being influenced by Satan. While they do have the ability to resist (I will address this in another section on Free Will), failing to do so results in exercising the desires of Satan. Remembering this will make it easier to forgive them for the pain and suffering they have caused you!

Finally, above all else, remember that in Christ you have victory in everything! You have victory over death.

You have victory over sin. You have victory over the world. You have victory over Satan. You have victory over anything and everything that sets itself up against the power of God:

> *When the perishable has been clothed with the imperishable, and the mortal with immortality, then the saying that is written will come true: "Death has been swallowed up in victory." "Where, O death, is your victory? Where, O death, is your sting?" The sting of death is sin, and the power of sin is the law. But thanks be to God! He gives us the victory through our Lord Jesus Christ. (1 Corinthians 15:54-57)*

# Understanding Prayer

I have been looking forward to writing this piece on understanding prayer for you. Prayer has been a major component of my life, as long as I can remember. I have always believed in God. I have always loved God, even if it was in my own misguided way. And, I have always prayed to God.

When it comes to prayer, I want you to have the correct mindset. I have often heard people say, "There is power in prayer!" In a way, I understand what they mean. On the other hand, however, I want you to learn correctly. So, to this statement I must say that it is inaccurate. I want you to learn from the beginning that there isn't power in prayer in and of itself. Rather, the power is in God. The power resides in and with God. However, with prayers and petitions we have access to God. The One who has the power. Now you may say, "This is a small and minor point!" Maybe. But, I believe it is important to make. If you don't have the correct understanding on this, you may begin to believe that there is power in prayer. Power just in speaking the words. Therefore, you may, over time, start to believe that things should happen in accordance with the prayers that you speak. This is not how prayer works.

Prayer is about talking to God. Prayer is about spending time with God. Prayer is about wanting to become like God, so that we imitate God. So that we think like God, and act like God. Remember, as a Christian, you now have a restored and reconciled relationship with God. When you are in a relationship with someone that you value, you will desire to spend time with that person. The same is true with God. Therefore, prayer should not be viewed as a means to an end. Prayer should not be viewed as the way we get things that we want from God. That isn't to say that we shouldn't ask God for the things that we want. I believe the Scriptures tell us to do that. However, when we start to treat God as a genie in a bottle, we have lost sight of the relationship component.

Please don't be afraid to pray! Look forward to times of prayer! Understand that in these times, God is working in you. Understand that time spent in prayer is time spent in the presence of God. Understand that in times of prayer you are being exposed to the character of God. In his first letter to the Corinthian church Paul made a very impactful statement regarding character. Check this out:

> **Do not be misled: "Bad company corrupts good character." (1 Corinthians 15:33)**

In this statement Paul is encouraging the Corinthian Christians to remember that they need to be on-guard concerning who they spend time with. Why is Paul telling them this? Because he knows and wants them to know and remember that it is very likely that they will become like the people that they spend time with. If you spend time with people that speak with profanity, then you are very likely to begin to speak with the same profanity. If you spend time with people that lie, cheat or steal; then you are likely to begin to do the same. In this particular case, Paul was addressing a growing number of people who were saying that Christ was not resurrected from the dead. Beyond that, they were saying, therefore; that no one will be resurrected from death to life. Paul was telling them that this line of thinking was false. That Christ was certainly resurrected from death to life, and that they needed to come back to the correct way of thinking. Back to the thinking that they had before being influenced by these people who were corrupted in their understanding. All this said, I hope that you learn to see prayer as spending time with a treasured friend. If you do, you will look forward to your times of prayer.

Ok, now I want to address for you making your requests known to God. Not only is this alright to do, but we are told to do it. God wants us to talk to Him, and He wants us to ask Him for the things that we want. This is what Paul wrote in Philippians Chapter 4:

> **Do not be anxious about anything, but in every situation, by prayer and petition, with thanksgiving, present your requests to God. (Philippians 4:6)**

God doesn't have a problem with us asking for things. This is not a problem at all. Things, however, become problematic when we lose our understanding of the relationship that we have with God. We are not in any position to make demands of God. Nor are we in any position to expect that God will grant each and every request that we put before Him. Remember that God is the creator, and we are the created. Keep in mind that God knows what you need, and what you want for that matter, even before you ask. No matter how badly you want something, God will never give you anything that is not good for you to have. Neither will He give you anything that you are not yet ready to handle. In this regard we can see how earthly fathers reflect the behavior of our heavenly Father.

In the same manner, remember that God wants to bless His children. He is ready, willing and able to bless you beyond your wildest imagination. Jesus put it like this:

> *"Which of you, if your son asks for bread, will give him a stone? Or if he asks for a fish, will give him a snake? If you, then, though you are evil, know how to give good gifts to your children, how much more will your Father in heaven give good gifts to those who ask him! (Matthew 7:9-11)*

The problem, therefore, is not in asking. Nor is it in receiving. Rather, however, there is a risk of a problem developing when you don't get what you want. When you begin to think that God is holding out on you. When you refuse to accept God's answer to prayer. And incidentally, a "No" is an answer to prayer. People, however, have developed a habit of saying that, "God didn't answer my prayer," when they don't get what they want. In actuality, God did answer their prayer. The answer was either "No" or "Not yet!" These are but a few of the responses we may receive from God as answers to prayer. In addition, God may grant the request, or give us something better than what we have asked. That's love! That's a great Father!

Prayer also speaks volumes on the position of your heart and the strength of your faith. When you pray, you are making a statement of faith. This is pleasing to God. For without faith, it impossible to please God. (Hebrews 11:6)

Prayer reveals that you understand and acknowledge that all matters in and of your life lie in the hands of God. That God is in control of all things! Prayer reveals your trust in the Lord (Proverbs 3:5-6), and your desire to allow the course of your life to be guided in His answers to your prayers.

So, keeping all of these things in mind, learn to pray. Yearn to pray. Live to pray. Love to pray, and pray as often as you can. In fact, pray continually. (1 Thessalonians 5:17)

Since prayer is about communication, there are no specific words that need to be said. There is no particular format. However, keep in mind that Jesus gave His disciples an example of how to pray. This was provided by Jesus in what is known as the "Sermon on the Mount." It was the greatest sermon ever preached, by the greatest preacher that ever lived. Here is what Jesus said about prayer to His disciples (Matthew 6:5-13):

> *"And when you pray, do not be like the hypocrites, for they love to pray standing in the synagogues and on the street corners to be seen by others. Truly I tell you, they have received their reward in full. But when you pray, go into your room, close the door and pray to your Father, who is unseen. Then your Father, who sees what is done in secret, will reward you. And when you pray, do not keep on babbling like pagans, for they think they will be heard because of their*

> *many words. Do not be like them, for your*
> *Father knows what you need before you ask him.*
> *"This, then, is how you should pray:*
> *"'Our Father in heaven, hallowed be your name,*
> *your kingdom come, your will be done, on earth*
> *as it is in heaven. Give us today our daily bread.*
> *And forgive us our debts, as we also have forgiven*
> *our debtors. And lead us not into temptation, but*
> *deliver us from the evil one.'*

These are the concepts of prayer. These are the things to keep in mind, as you pray. These are the building blocks of your communing with the Father. These are not, however, the exact words that need to be said each and every time that you pray. On the other hand, however, there is nothing wrong with praying these words whenever you want. I want you to remember not to be bound up with the mechanics or the technicalities of prayer. God is more concerned about your heart, than the eloquence of which you speak. Therefore, do not develop a legalistic by-the-book outlook concerning prayer. If you do, you will miss all that prayer is supposed to be for and to you! If you love God, then you will love to pray. In prayer, you draw near to God; and He draws near to you.

> *Submit yourselves, then, to God. Resist the*
> *devil, and he will flee from you. Come near to*
> *God and he will come near to you. (James 4:7-8)*

Finally, I want you to understand that as a Christian, prayer is your most effective weapon in spiritual warfare. Prayer is how you fight against the enemy! Whether it be the devil or a person being influenced by the devil, prayer should always be your weapon of choice. Look at this:

> *For though we (Christians) live in the world, we do not wage war as the world does. The weapons we fight with are not the weapons of the world. On the contrary, they have divine power to demolish strongholds. We demolish arguments and every pretension that sets itself up against the knowledge of God, and we take captive every thought to make it obedient to Christ. (2 Corinthians 10:3-5)*

Attending Worship Services

Attending worship services with other Christians is very important, and part of God's plan for the church. Imagine if one of your relatives was hosting a large family gathering, but many members of the family that were invited stayed home. Let's say that they thought they could get the same benefit alone; as they could get from meeting with everyone else in the family. You can see that this type of thinking is quite foolish. How could they possibly get the same benefit when they miss the event? They can't! However, in addition to being foolish it is also selfish. When people try to live their Christian lives as "Lone Rangers," for a host of reasons, they fail to see that they are being selfish. In this way of thinking, they are only focused on themselves. They are only focused on what they need. I understand that there isn't anything wrong with a person focusing on their own needs and interests. But, the Bible tells us to think outside of ourselves. Here is how Paul put it in Philippians:

> *Do nothing out of selfish ambition or vain conceit. Rather, in humility value others above yourselves, not looking to your own interests but each of you to the interests of the others. (Philippians 2:3-4)*

So, then, when we isolate ourselves from other members of the church; we are neglecting the interests of others in the church. Try to remember that other people need you. They need to hear your words of encouragement. They need to see your faith in action. They need your prayers in times of struggle. They need you in their lives. One of the things that has really impacted me during the course of my illness is how so many people in the church have been strengthened and encouraged each time that I am present for worship, even though I have a terminal illness.

There are, of course, many other reasons that you should attend worship services with other Christians. In these times, you will learn and grow together. In these times, you will be sharing your faith together. You will be strengthening and encouraging each other. And, perhaps most important of all, you will be taking the Lord's Supper together.

If you truly love God, then you will truly love God's children. You will love God's Family. You will desire to worship with the family. You will desire to have times of fellowship with the family. And, you will desire to serve with the family!

Finally, remember this from God's Word:

> *Let us hold unswervingly to the hope we profess, for he who promised is faithful. And let us consider how we may spur one another on toward love and good deeds, not giving up meeting together, as some are in the habit of doing, but encouraging one another—and all the more as you see the Day approaching. (Hebrews 10:23-25)*

Remember that when you attend worship services you are joining in a family gathering, and it is a wonderful experience. It is something that you should enjoy, treasure and want to do every week.

There are many reasons that people give for not attending worship. I have heard many of them. Don't make excuses for failing to do what you know you should do. Rather, admit that you did wrong, and move in the direction of doing right! Out of all the excuses, however, that are given, the worst ones are when people use the event of the worship service itself as a reason for not attending. They say things like; "I don't like the preacher," or "The song leader isn't going to be good today." And countless others. I hope you realize how bad this is, without me saying it, as you read this yourself. Oh yeah, and here's the worst one of all, "I have to work!"

All of these indicate a big problem. They indicate a heart problem. They indicate that the one thinking and saying such things is focused on themselves, rather than on God. Remember that worship service is never about the one giving the worship. Worship is about the One receiving the worship. It's about honoring God in all the ways that He has declared. Worshipping God is not about what you get out of the experience. Please remember it is not about getting. It is about giving. Worship is about giving God thanks. It's about giving God glory. It's about honoring God and recognizing Him, and all that He continues to do for you. Why do we think everything is always supposed to be about us? In worship, we get out of ourselves. In worship we focus on God, which is the best thing to do. So, get off that high-horse of everything being about you; and get on with being about God. By the way, it has been my experience that when I have the right attitude, worship is an amazing experience. On the other hand, when I have had the wrong attitude, worship doesn't seem to fulfill me. Imagine that! Make sure that you don't develop a critical spirit! If you do, you will always be displeased and unsatisfied.

There is another aspect to remember about worship. Whatever you truly worship, you will give yourself over to. If you love God, you will worship God. Or, in other words, you will give yourself over to God. You will spend your time and money on God and doing godly things. If you love your job, you will devote much of your time, effort and energy to your job. It is good to work hard, and to have a reputation as a diligent worker. This is important to God. But worshipping God is more important to God than how you do on the job. Your worship of God is more important than getting a promotion, a raise or some extra dollars in your next paycheck. Besides that, if you are a child of God, God will meet your needs.

Now I want to address the working on Sunday issue. There is a balance that needs to be considered here. By the way, this is yet another indicator of how our culture has changed over the years. When I was a kid, growing up in the 60s and 70s, there was hardly any type of store or business open on Sunday. Sunday was a holy day. God's day. It was understood that people were going to spend the morning worshipping God, and then being with family. I can remember that we actually had to make sure that we had everything that we needed on Saturday, because on Sunday you couldn't get it. That even included making sure that there was gas in the car. Yes, there were some gas stations open; but they were few and far between. Okay, that's it with the flashback! Anyway, here is what I want you to remember. Yes, you need to work. Yes, you need to earn money. And, yes, you need to provide for your family. That is a Biblical mandate. However, if there is any way possible for you to accomplish these things without working Sunday on a regular basis do it.

Now there are many people that will tell you that it is not necessary to gather with the church, to worship God. Amen and hallelujah, that is so true! I couldn't agree more. In fact, what we do Monday thru Saturday in our daily lives is a crucial part of our worship. Remember the point about giving yourself over to the things you worship. Well, that's what makes this statement true. Usually, however, when people say this they aren't really trying to make a Biblical point. No, typically, they are trying to rationalize their refusal and rebellion pertaining to attending worship services with other Christians. Paul noted this issue of giving of yourself as worship in his letter to the Roman churches:

> *Therefore, I urge you, brothers and sisters, in view of God's mercy, to offer your bodies as a living sacrifice, holy and pleasing to God—this is your true and proper worship. (Romans 12:1)*

So, then, what you do Monday thru Saturday, and how you do it is definitely important; and can be an act of worship. However, this should never be used as an excuse or a reason for not attending worship on Sunday with other Christians. Again, it comes down to the heart.

If you value God, and His children; then you will attend. It is NOT all about you!

Therefore, if you ever have any questions on what you value, or what is truly important to you there is an easy and very revealing way to tell. Look back through your calendar and your checkbook. The answers lie in how you are spending your time and your money.

Please make attending worship services a priority in your life for your entire life!

God's Family

Being part of a loving, caring and godly family is a beautiful thing. That is what you gain, when you are a Christian. As a Christian you become part of God's Family. You become part of the family of believers.

While Christians are supposed to be kind and generous to everyone, and I hope that you will be, there is an extra measure of love and kindness that Christians are supposed to extend to one another. Paul indicates this in his letter to the churches in Galatia:

> *Therefore, as we have opportunity, let us do good to all people, especially to those who belong to the family of believers. (Galatians 6:10)*

I want you to know that all through my Christian life, but especially in my illness with cancer, the Family of God has been amazing. In 2017, Marti and I have received love, care, compassion, prayer support and generosity beyond measure. God's people from each of the three congregations (especially the congregation of Laurel, Maryland) of which we have been members, have poured themselves out to us in ways that truly blessed us. Beyond that, however, we had Christians from other congregations all over the world praying for us. This is what you get when you are part of God's Family!

Christians share and experience a special bond. It is the bond of Christ. It is the bond of love. The bond of holiness. The bond of righteousness, and forgiveness. Therefore, Christians should behave in a loving and caring way towards other Christians.

Paul wrote this in his letter to the churches in Colossae:

> *Therefore, as God's chosen people, holy and dearly loved, clothe yourselves with compassion, kindness, humility, gentleness and patience. Bear with each other and forgive one another if any of you has a grievance against someone. Forgive as the Lord forgave you. And over all these virtues put on love, which binds them all together in perfect unity. (Colossians 3:12-14)*

Always remember that when you are among Christians, you are among family. Wherever you go, and you find the Lord's church you are among family – God's Family!

As part of God's Family, strive to do your best to be the member you should be. Nonetheless, in spite of your best efforts, remember that you will fail at times. You will hurt people's feelings. You will let them down. You will say and do things that you shouldn't. You will neglect to say and do things that you should. You may cause problems that impact the entire family. When this happens, you will want to be forgiven. So, admit your shortcomings. Tell the ones that you hurt that you are sorry. And, ask to be forgiven.

Always remember that your relationships with other members of God's Family hinge on and are dependent upon your relationship with God. Getting right and staying right with God is based on admitting sin, being sorry about sin and seeking forgiveness. It is the same with the relationships that you develop with other members of God's Family, and with anyone else for that matter.

If you want to develop and maintain healthy relationships with other people, especially the members of God's Family, keep in mind these nine words when you blow it:

I was wrong.

I am sorry.

Please forgive me.

If you can't bring yourself to say these nine words to God, and to other people, then you are already beginning to put your relationships in jeopardy! Please don't let your pride get in the way. Swallow it. Do the right thing! You will be surprised how much this will strengthen your relationships!

Character and Integrity

Character and integrity seem to be qualities of days and times gone by. They seem to be passé. They are not really valued. I can't say why for sure. However, people these days seem to be more concerned with what they get, more than who they are. This is sad, and speaks volumes about the current state of the culture of America. I believe that we need a revival in our nation on all things God, but especially with regard to godly values. If you study the cultural changes that have affected our nation over the last fifty or sixty years, I am certain that you will come to the same conclusion.

Therefore, character and integrity are very important to me, and I hope that they will be important to you. More importantly, however, character and integrity are very important to God. God wants and expects His children to represent Him well. If you become a child of God, and I pray that you will, then you will be deemed a representative of Jesus here on earth. In essence, the Bible says that Christians are ambassadors for Christ. (2 Corinthians 5:20).

An ambassador represents the one who has appointed them, to go to places they cannot go. They go bringing the message of the one that they represent. They go emulating the beliefs and values of the one that they represent. They are to speak and convey only as they have been authorized by the one that they represent. That said, I hope that you can see how the mission of every Christian is so important. Please don't ever underestimate the importance of your place in this world, but especially as you are here as an ambassador of Christ. As a Christian, you have been given a mandate by Jesus. This is what Jesus told His disciples to do, before ascending to heaven:

> *Then Jesus came to them and said, "All authority in heaven and on earth has been given to me. Therefore go and make disciples of all nations, baptizing them in the name of the Father and of the Son and of the Holy Spirit, and teaching them to obey everything I have commanded you. And surely I am with you always, to the very end of the age." (Matthew 28:18-20)*

Making disciples, teaching and baptizing is what all Christians should strive to do. But, remember that the kind of person that you are will have a significant impact on how people receive the message about Jesus that you bring. People will be more open to what you have to say about Christ, if they see and know that you are acting like Christ. As the cliché goes, "You can talk the talk, but are you walking the walk?" If you want to impact the world with Jesus, then you must live like Jesus, be like Jesus and look like Jesus. Among other things, that means being a person of character and integrity.

It has been said that the character of a person can be determined by what they do, when they believe that no one is watching them. In some ways this is a good definition. We are who we are when we think no one is able to see us. Noble character is genuine character. It is not faked. It is not a false front that is displayed to achieve a desired goal.

I hope that you will strive to develop godly character traits as you are shaped and molded by the working of the Holy Spirit. In Paul's letter to the churches in Rome, Paul addresses the issue of character development. Here is part of what he wrote:

> *Therefore, since we have been justified through faith, we have peace with God through our Lord Jesus Christ, through whom we have gained access by faith into this grace in which we now stand. And we boast in the hope of the glory of God. Not only so, but we also glory in our sufferings, because we know that suffering produces perseverance; perseverance, character; and character, hope. And hope does not put us to shame, because God's love has been poured out into our hearts through the Holy Spirit, who has been given to us. (Romans 5:1-5)*

Remember that as a child of God, God is working to conform you into the image of Christ. He wants you to look like Jesus to a lost, dark and dying world. He wants you to be the kind of person that can be trusted. That can be relied upon. That can be counted on to speak the truth! Along with what I have written here study the book of James. You need to understand that in suffering and trials God is building your character, and conforming you into the person He wants you to be for Him. I know this is tough stuff! I know it may be hard to understand, but again that is part of the character building process. Just keep reading, and studying and praying. You will begin to see the light!

Always seek truth. Always desire truth. Always strive to be a person of character and integrity for Jesus.

The Complexities of
Understanding Free Will

T he subject of free will has been something that has confused many people for many years. Sadly, it has even confused many Christians. Understanding free will, however, is not really that complicated; as long as your beginning reference point is correct. What I mean by that is that you have to state some underlying facts. If you do this, things become much clearer and easier to see. Let me explain! First of all, begin with the fact that God is sovereign. That means that God is in control of everything. Yes, I mean everything. God is control of all events that happen in your life, in the lives of your family members and in the lives of every person that you know and all that you don't. That said, you need to understand that being in control does not mean that God intervenes in every aspect of our lives. I will use an analogy that you will be able to relate to, at some point in your life. Before I became a minster of the gospel I was an engineering manager. In my positions of authority, I had direct control over many employees. I was in control of their work. I was in control of their performance reviews. I was in control of who they worked with, their hours of work, what projects they worked on, etc. Yet, as their manager, I did not necessarily intervene in every area of their work life. I could have, and often did; but I didn't do so in every case. This is the point that I am making with God. Even though God has the power and the ability to intervene in every aspect of every person's life any minute of any day, that does not mean that He will or that He has to do so.

As an aside, there is another thing to remember which should help and encourage you. God is even in control of Satan. I will explain this more in the section titled, "God Tests, and Satan Tempts." Therefore, Satan cannot do anything with you or to you, that God does not permit. Anyway, back to the subject at hand. So, keeping this fact in mind we move on.

God created people to be in relationship with Him. He created us out of the love within Him. He created us to love us, and to love Him back in return. He could control us, and force us to love Him, but that would not please Him or bring Him glory. Again, I will use an analogy to explain this to you. Godly parents love their children. They want their children to love them. It is very pleasing to them when their children hug and kiss them. While they could force their children to hug and kiss them, especially when they are little, they don't (okay at least not that much). Why is this the case? Because the times that they force their children to display love to them it's not the same. It doesn't illicit the same reaction in them that occurs when their children do it because they want to do it. In essence, what is happening here is that the parents are in control of their children; but they give their children free will to express their love how and when they want. This is the same thing with God. God is in control of His children, but He gives His children free will to do what they want. The case we are using is applicable in the case of expressing love. By the way, we see that in so many aspects of life. Consider a marriage proposal. When a man proposes to a woman one of the things that makes it so special is that he is asking a lot of her. When she says yes, on her own, without any type of coercion; it makes him the happiest man in the world. So, we see another very important thing here which leads to the next conditional statement. Love allows for and makes room for choice. During the times of vacationing in Ocean City, Maryland with our family we would walk along the boardwalk. We loved to sample the various treats, and look at all the different things that could be purchased. There were always a number of clothing vendors. I remember seeing a T-shirt one year that really impacted me. It said, "If you love something set it free. If it comes back, it's yours. If it doesn't, it never was." I thought that was a great way to define how love acts. Real love allows the freedom of choice. The same is true with God. God really loves the people that He creates, so much so that He gives everyone of them the choice of loving Him back, or not. I hope and pray that you choose to love God back.

So, I hope that you are getting a clearer picture on the issue of free will. There is, however, another aspect to consider on this issue. While God extends free will to people, it doesn't mean that their free will is limitless. Let me explain. Let's say that someone desires to hurt you. They may even decide to kill you. Well, imagine that, that's exactly what happened to Jesus. People tried to kill him a number of times. Jesus, however, was not killed by them. No, on the contrary, He slipped away somehow and lived to preach and teach another day. Why? Simply put, God chose to intervene to protect His Son in these particular cases. It was not the will of God for Jesus to die at the hands of these people when they wanted to kill Him. Oh, they really wanted to kill Jesus, no doubt about it. But, they were not able to do it. Their free will was overruled by the will of God. Now some people may argue against this logic, because it involves Jesus. I would say that it doesn't matter. The way God reacted in the life of Jesus, is the same way that God reacts in the lives of all people. There are certain things that God will prevent other people from doing, because their actions do not align with His will.

On the other hand, when it was the right time for Jesus to go to the cross; neither Jesus Himself or the Father intervened in any way to keep Him from being crucified. Actually, it was just the opposite. Both Father and Son knew that the crucifixion was necessary, and they wanted it to happen. This is another case where we see true love making a choice. Jesus could have prevented Himself from being crucified. He was moved by His love for the Father so much, that He chose to go to the cross. People often say that Jesus went to the cross because He loves us. That's true! But, I think that the thing that really pushed Him was His love for the Father. We should learn a lot from His love for the Father. Always remember this situation involving Jesus:

> *Then he (Jesus) said to them (the disciples),*
> *My soul is overwhelmed with sorrow to the point*
> *of death.*
> *Stay here and keep watch with me."*
> *Going a little farther, he fell with his face to the*
> *ground and prayed,*

"My Father, if it is possible, may this cup be taken from me. Yet not as I will, but as you will." (Matthew 26:38-39)

Jesus knew what He was facing. He could have stopped it, but He didn't. He asked His Father to stop it, but He didn't. Jesus was okay with this, because He desired His Father's will to be done over His will. This is the model for all Christians to understand and follow.

As a Christian, you will know that you are really maturing and experiencing growth spurts when you desire the will of God to be done, over your will, in and with your life.

It has always been interesting to me how people want free will to do what they want, when they want, as much as they want and with whom they want; but then expect God to intervene when things don't turn out the way they wanted. We are a most peculiar people!

Sex, Sexual Addiction and Pornography

Before I get into this specific topic I want you to know that this material is applicable to both male and female readers. While written to help my two grandsons understand the implications of these issues, it will also be helpful to the opposite sex. An increasing amount of the female population has been developing a sexual addiction. And even if you don't have a sexual addiction yourself, you should be aware of the impact that this type of addiction has on people. After all, you may be dating or married to such a person right now - or in the future. And by the way, you need to understand that an addiction to pornography is a sexual addiction. In addition, please be advised and take the issues of sex, sexual addiction and pornography seriously. These issues have the potential to mess up your mind, life and future.

> *"The youth of America is ill equipped to make good decisions for themselves with regard to the issues of viewing pornographic material. They have no concept or idea of just how damaging and far-reaching their decisions will have on their lives, or on the lives of the people they love."*
>
> Ian J. Drucker

You need to know and remember that sex is a gift from God. God created people, male and female, and chose the act of sexual intercourse for the means of reproducing. There is immense pleasure and intimacy in the act of sexual intercourse. Unfortunately, however, this gift of God has been corrupted by the enemy of God (Satan), and the desires of ungodly people.

When I was 13 years-old I viewed some Playboy magazines. That initial exposure grew into an addiction that lasted 29 years. This addiction led to the destruction of my first marriage, and almost to the demise of my second marriage. The thing about having an addiction, any addiction, that I want you to be aware of is that eventually the addiction will consume your life. It is not a matter of if, but rather a matter of when. It is interesting how doing something that I thought would make me feel like a man ultimately made me feel anything but manly.

As a man, you need to have the utmost respect for women. They are great treasures! If you have a misguided ungodly view of sex, you will develop an incorrect and disgraceful opinion of women. You will see them as objects (sex objects) to be used for your own pleasure. Over time, they will become void of emotions, feelings and values to you. You will fail to see them as creatures of God, and you will fall to the temptation of pure objectification. Therefore, don't ever use women or sex as a way of making you feel better about yourself. If you think that this is what you need to do to feel better, seek out and find a godly counselor immediately. In addition, do not view sexual encounters as any type of conquest marking your transition into manhood. This way of thinking is nothing like being a real man. Being a real man, is being a man of God!

At the time of my writing this book, there have been a number of men of prominence and notoriety who have admitted committing sexual harassment against women whom they worked with, and had power over. Make certain you stay clear of anything even close to this type of behavior. Paul reminds Christians of this very important stance on the issue of sexual immorality:

> *But among you there must not be even a hint of sexual immorality, or of any kind of impurity, or of greed, because these are improper for God's holy people. (Ephesians 5:3)*

The Bible gives us clear instruction regarding how Christian men are to treat women. Paul wrote to the young minister Timothy, his son in the faith, advising him to treat older women as mothers, and younger women as sisters, with absolute purity. (1 Timothy 5:2)

I advise every Christian man, which I hope and pray that you will become, to do the same. If you want to attain a godly woman as a mate, then you must really be a godly man. The key here is that you need to really be a godly man, and not just give the false appearance of being godly.

If you want to have a healthy marriage that meets the needs of your wife, then you will need to have the proper understanding of her as a woman. Anything that you do, or anything that you indulge in, that involves sexual sin will erode your ability to do this. In addition to this, getting involved with sexual sin is your invitation to Satan for him to attack you with a barrage of temptations that will be hard for you to stave off.

Surely, even while you are without sin in this area, Satan will be tempting you to indulge in sexual immorality and sin. The temptations can and will come in many forms. Satan will also use people in your life such as friends, classmates, people at work and even people in your own family to encourage you to indulge in sexual sin and/or the viewing of pornographic material. DON'T FALL TO THE TEMPTATION!

In your resistance to view pornography or to indulge in other forms of sexual sin, people may make fun of you. Let them. These people, especially so-called friends, will be nowhere to be found when you and your mate are undergoing marriage counselling due to your addictive behavior.

Remember that every woman that you view and use as a sex object is someone's daughter, or may be someone's mother, or wife or sister.

Sexual fulfillment was given by God, and was intended strictly for the marriage bed.

I tell you these things, not only because they are true – and they are, but also because I love you. I want to spare you the same pain, suffering and embarrassment that I experienced due to my addiction to pornography.

I thank God that I was delivered from my addiction, by the power of the Holy Spirit. This came after I cried out to God, at a men's retreat, admitting my sinfulness (in the Fall of 2002). It wasn't long after this event that I felt God's call on my life to become a minster of the gospel. I eventually responded to the call, and I have remained a minister of the gospel to this day (December 22, 2017).

I know that guarding your heart and mind from impure thoughts in the area of sexuality can be difficult.

Nonetheless, however, it is what the Scriptures command us to do:

> *We demolish arguments and every pretension*
> *that sets itself up against the knowledge of God,*
> *and we take captive every thought to make it*
> *obedient to Christ. (2 Corinthians 10:5)*

I want you to understand the nature of pornography addiction. It is for your own good that I am going into such detail on a very sensitive issue. Porn addiction is insidious. It creeps up on people. Well, it crept up on me at least. I have learned a lot about addiction and addictive behavior in the 29 years that I struggled with my addiction to porn. I also gained a lot of knowledge in trying to help other men break free from this same addiction.

One of the most significant realizations that I came to was that when you begin to feed an addiction you are creating a monster. In this case I was creating a "Porn Monster" within me.

There was a man named Nicodemus who came to visit the Lord one night. He had a very interesting conversation with the Lord. One of the most intriguing things that Jesus said to Nicodemus is recorded for us in the gospel of John, as follows:

> *Flesh gives birth to flesh, but the Spirit gives*
> *birth to spirit. (John 3:6)*

This is a crucial statement and applies not only to being born again of God's Holy Spirit, but also has a practical implication on how we live our lives. I didn't realize the essence of this until I was freed from my addiction, and I was teaching Bible classes in the Frederick County Detention Center near my home. Here's the thing. When we sin yielding to the flesh, we are in essence feeding the flesh (this grieves the Holy Spirit within us). This in turn increases the desires of our flesh. Likewise, when we do godly things (motivated by the influence of the Holy Spirit in us) then we are feeding the spirit. We are in essence yielding to the Spirit.

The apostle Paul also made this distinction in his letter to the churches in Galatia.

> *So I say, walk by the Spirit, and you will not gratify the desires of the flesh.*
> *For the flesh desires what is contrary to the Spirit, and the Spirit what is contrary to the flesh.*
> *They are in conflict with each other, so that you are not to do whatever you want. (Galatians 5:16-17)*

There is a critical element that needs to be discussed here. Notice what Paul says. It is not unusual, and it should not be surprising that we have the desire to sin within us. In the same way we need to understand that being tempted to sin is not a sin in and of itself. The sin occurs when we yield to the temptation and we do what our flesh desires, rather than what the Spirit of God desires (thus grieving the Spirit). God wants His people to be pure. That is to be Holy. And remember that even when we are being tempted, God is at work for us. We can never be tempted beyond our ability to stand-up under the temptation. For God would not allow that. Satan can only tempt us as he is permitted by God. This is shown to us in the account of Job. In addition, this matter is clarified in the New Testament as well:

> **No temptation has overtaken you except what is common to mankind. And God is faithful; he will not let you be tempted beyond what you can bear. But when you are tempted, he will also provide a way out so that you can endure it. (1 Corinthians 10:13)**

So, then, when facing temptation teach and train yourself to rely on the faithfulness of God and take the way out. Sadly, too many times the temptation is yielded to and then the grace and mercy of God is relied upon. This should not be the case!

When we give-in to the desire to look at porn we are giving birth to "The Porn Monster." As we continue to sin by looking at porn, we are growing "The Porn Monster." The most important thing I learned about "The Porn Monster" is that it has an insatiable appetite. Once you start feeding it, it can never get enough. It needs to eat constantly. But worse than that, even while it is feeding it is already looking forward to its next feeding session.

So, realize and understand that in time "The Porn Monster" will consume your life. It is not a matter of if; it is a matter of when. It will consume you! You can and you may make all kinds of rationalizations; but the fact is that it will dominate you. But here is another interesting facet of "The Porn Monster." Once it is done with you it reaches out and starts affecting everyone in your life. Its tentacles reach out and touch those around you. It is amazing to me how people stuck in addiction are convinced that their behavior doesn't affect anyone else. This is a lie, and a rationalization that is typically employed to make the addict feel better about their behavior. As the monster grows within, you end up living your life to serve your addiction rather than God. The monster grows, and over time loved ones are sacrificed – when Christians are supposed to sacrifice themselves. Consequently, God's desires are not met. The apostle Paul addressed this issue with the Christians in Rome, as follows:

> *Therefore, I urge you, brothers and sisters, in view of God's mercy, to offer your bodies as a living sacrifice, holy and pleasing to God—this is your true and proper worship. Do not conform to the pattern of this world, but be transformed by the renewing of your mind. Then you will be able to test and approve what God's will is— his good, pleasing and perfect will. (Romans 12:1-2)*

Christians are called to offer their bodies as a sacrifice to God. They are supposed to live a holy life, which pleases God, and not behave like most people – whom do not know God. To be holy and pleasing to God is to worship the Lord God, and serve Him over self and anything else. As the monster is fed and grows, a change in focus occurs. The focus becomes living a life of selfishness. Everything turns to being about self, and on feeding the flesh. Everything is about feeding the addiction. Oh, you may be able to function. You may be able to hold a job. You may even be earning money in a chosen field, but in the background the monster is very active. The monster is healthy and growing stronger day by day.

I took very good care of my monster. It was the first thing that I thought about every day when I woke up. I didn't think about thanking God for another day. I didn't think about thanking God for all the blessings that I had in my life. I didn't think about all the things that I should have been thinking about. No, instead, I thought about taking care of my monster. I was very concerned about how I would feed it that day. In my mind, I ran through my schedule. I tried to recall what my wife had told me about her schedule for that day. I would begin to formulate in my mind how and when to feed my monster. I became a very good caretaker. I became very creative. Some days I would provide feedings in the form of the internet. Other days I would go to a strip club. Other days I would do both.

Above all else, the most important thing I can say about the monster is that once it has been conceived it is very difficult to slay. It doesn't die easily. And there will likely be times that you believe you have killed it, only to find that it is still alive within you. However, don't lose hope! The monster can be killed. The writer of Ecclesiastes offers some very encouraging words.

> *Anyone who is among the living has hope –*
> *even a live dog is better off than a dead lion!*
> *(Ecclesiastes 9:4)*

Dating and Marriage

Dating and deciding on a mate will be one of the most exciting and challenging things you will ever undertake. To be successful in these areas there are some key things you need to know. And while we are at it, allow me to explain what I mean by being successful. Success as I use the term is quite different from the way you may have thought about it most of your life. When I talk about success, in any regard, I am talking about doing something in a way that is pleasing to God. Most people think about success in worldly terms. Do not adopt this way of thinking, it will lead to much confusion and heartache. Always think about and frame success in terms of godly actions, behaviors and outcomes. Nothing is more important than doing things God's way. I learned this the hard way. Again, I am trying to spare you from making some of the same mistakes that I have made. I know that you need to live your own life. I know that you need to make some of your own mistakes. That is necessary for you to become the person that God wants you to be. However, my goal here is to help insure that you don't make any life-long mistakes. Don't be stubborn like I was for a great part of my life. I thought that I knew a lot more than I really did. I thought I knew God, without accepting Christ. I was wrong! That can't be done. I was living life my way, and it seemed right. Later on, I found out that there was a Proverb that addressed this very issue. It is Proverbs 14:12, which reads:

> *There is a way that appears to be right, but in the end it leads to death.*

You cannot know what is true, right and good without knowing what God has said about such things. That is why it is so important to know the word of God, "The Holy Bible." Paul and Peter address the issue of living to please God in a number of ways. Here is one place where Paul addresses this issue:

> *For you were once darkness, but now you are light in the Lord. Live as children of light (for the fruit of the light consists in all goodness, righteousness and truth) and find out what pleases the Lord. (Ephesians 5:8-10)*

The purpose of dating is to get to know someone, period! It is not to find a sex partner. It is not to have someone with whom you can fulfill your sexual desires and/or impulses.

Learn this, focus on this and pray about this! Dating is something that you should do to really get to know someone. And be on-guard, for many people can fake who they really are for a long time. Therefore, you need to date someone for a long enough time for the person to show their true colors. The process of dating and mate selection is tough enough, even with "true love." If you introduce the emotional intimacy that occurs in the act of sexual intercourse into your relationship before you are married, you have not only sinned against God; but you have also succeeded in impairing your judgement and your ability to see the other person as they really are. This is a big reason that God deems the gift of sex for the marital relationship. During sexual intercourse there is an emotional intimacy that occurs that is amazing and captivating. This is part of God's design in joining a husband and wife in a life-long bond. You are asking for trouble anytime you act in conflict with the will, plan and purpose of God in and for your life.

Dating provides the opportunity to have fun together, and to learn about each other. In dating, make sure you see the person in all the circumstances of everyday life. Make sure you see how a person handles stress, money, adversity, disappointment and success. Make sure that you are able to see how the person really is, and not just the person that they want you to see.

Most of all, however, make sure you have enough time to be certain that the person whom you are dating truly loves the Lord. Okay, there, I said it! Hoping and expecting that you will be a Christian by the time you start dating, be certain that the people that you date are also Christians. Now wait a second, before you go off the deep end, remember what I said. Everything that I am telling you I am telling you because I love you. I am not telling you these things to control you, to hamper your fun or for any other thing that you may be thinking. This is similar to all the reasons that God tells us what we should do, and what we shouldn't do. God created us. He knows the things that are good for us, as well as the things that are bad for us. He wants us to avoid pain and sorrow to the greatest possible extent. Much of the time, we create our own crisis!

When you make an exception to start dating a non-Christian, you are opening the door to experience heartache and sorrow. Yes, there is always the possibility that the person may convert in time. On the other hand, there is always the possibility that they won't. Therein lies the problem. Therein lies the conflict. I have known many people who dated and later married non-Christians, thinking that they could convert them; only to spend their lives in service to the Lord competing with the selfish desires of ungodly mates. Consider these words from the apostle Paul concerning marriage between believers:

> *But a married man is concerned about the affairs of this world—how he can please his wife— and his interests are divided. An unmarried woman or virgin is concerned about the Lord's affairs: Her aim is to be devoted to the Lord in both body and spirit. But a married woman is concerned about the affairs of this world—how she can please her husband. I am saying this for your own good, not to restrict you, but that you may live in a right way in undivided devotion to the Lord. (1 Corinthians 7:33-35)*

Because of having divided interests once married, it is better for people to remain single. On the other hand, however, it is better to marry than to burn with passion. Therefore, a godly marriage is pleasing to the Lord. The point that I am making here is that it is difficult enough to please the Lord when you are married to a believer. Trying to do it being married to a non-believer, is close to impossible. You can avoid the pain of this situation by never dating a non-believer.

Now, you may be asking, "Does that mean that I can never have a close friend of the opposite sex who is a non-believer?" The answer is, "Of course not!" However, you must take extra precautions to guard your heart, and realize that Satan will use everyone and anyone he can to steal you away from the Lord. Such issues are addressed in the Chapter on Spiritual Warfare. This doesn't mean that the person in and of themselves is evil. Rather a person without the Holy Spirit of God is often unable to see, realize or understand how Satan is using them to do his will. Consider these words that Paul wrote to Timothy on this issue:

> *Opponents (non-believers) must be gently instructed, in the hope that God will grant them repentance leading them to a knowledge of the truth, and that they will come to their senses and escape from the trap of the devil, who has taken them captive to do his will. (2 Timothy 2:25-26)*

Now back to having a close friend of the opposite sex. Well, my wife is my best friend. This past July, 2017, we celebrated our 27th Wedding Anniversary.

My hope and my prayer for you is that you are able to marry your best friend. Don't settle for less, just to get married. Make sure that your relationship with your future mate is amazing. Make sure that your future mate isn't just someone that you can live with. Rather, make sure your future mate is someone that you can't live without. That's what I have had with Marti, my beautiful wife, all of these years. There is nothing wrong with the draw of physical attraction, we had it, but don't ever let it be all that pulls you together. And remember that:

> *Your beauty (the beauty of a wife) should not*
> *come from outward adornment, such as elaborate*
> *hairstyles and the wearing of gold jewelry or fine*
> *clothes. Rather, it should be that of your inner*
> *self, the unfading beauty of a gentle and quiet*
> *spirit, which is of great worth in God's sight.*
> *(1 Peter 3:3-4)*

Also remember, that any relationship which is worth maintaining takes work and effort. Your relationship with God will take time and effort. You will need to read the Bible, pray and live a life striving to honor God. Your marriage, likewise, will take work and effort. Don't ever put your marriage on auto-pilot thinking it can guide itself, it can't. Make sure that you lead, guide and love your wife every day of your life. She should know without any doubt that she is the most important woman in the world to you. Your mother has a place in your life, of course, but she should never be placed in higher regard than your wife.

It should be the same with your relationship with God. Don't ever let your wife, or anyone else, displace your love for Christ. I can still remember the day I was walking with my mother in the courtyard of the nursing home in which she was living. My wife and I were Christians, but my mother was still clinging to her Jewish roots; failing to see Jesus as the Son of God. As we were walking I said something about how beautiful the surroundings were, and I began to make a reference to Jesus as the creator of all things. I knew this from my study of the gospel of John, specifically Chapter 1. Anyway, my mother grabbed my hands with her hands. She stood right in front of me, and looked me right in the eyes. Then she said the words I will never forget! She said, "This is the last time that you will ever speak to me about Jesus. That's it, I don't ever want to hear about him again." I answered her quietly and as gently as I could. I replied, "Okay mom, but if you ever force me to make a choice between you and Jesus, you need to know that I will pick Jesus." I know that these words were tough for my mother to hear, but I believe in my heart of hearts that they were wonderful words to the ears of our Lord. Always remember these words spoken by Jesus:

> *"Anyone who loves their father or mother more than me is not worthy of me; anyone who loves their son or daughter more than me is not worthy of me." (Matthew 10:37)*

You will need to increase your knowledge about your wife. You will need to learn what kind of things mean love to her. This is called, "Understanding Her Love Language." There are many books which have been written on this topic. However, I recommend that you read a book by Gary Chapman. It is titled, "The Five Love Languages: How to Express Heartfelt Commitment to Your Mate."

Make sure that your wife never has any doubt that you love her. Incidentally, you should do the same with anyone that you love and value.

Marriage vows are sacred before God. Honor them with all of your heart. Be true to your wife. Be careful that you don't develop a wandering eye or heart. Remember these words from Jesus:

> *"You have heard that it was said, 'You shall not commit adultery.' But I tell you that anyone who looks at a woman lustfully has already committed adultery with her in his heart. If your right eye causes you to stumble, gouge it out and throw it away. It is better for you to lose one part of your body than for your whole body to be thrown into hell. (Matthew 5:27-29)*

One final thing, on the subject of marriage, don't ever believe that homosexuality or same-sex marriage is a good thing. Regardless of what people say, and they say a lot - even when they shouldn't, know and understand that same-sex marriage and homosexuality are detestable to God. There are many Scriptures that indicate that God detests homosexual practices. Here is one in particular:

> *We also know that the law is made not for the righteous but for lawbreakers and rebels, the ungodly and sinful, the unholy and irreligious, for those who kill their fathers or mothers, for murderers, for the sexually immoral, for those practicing homosexuality, for slave traders and liars and perjurers—and for whatever else is contrary to the sound doctrine that conforms to the gospel concerning the glory of the blessed God, which he entrusted to me. (1 Timothy 1:9-11)*

In addition:

> *Because of this, God gave them over to shameful lusts. Even their women exchanged natural sexual relations for unnatural ones. In the same way the men also abandoned natural relations with women and were inflamed with lust for one another. Men committed shameful acts with other men, and received in themselves the due penalty for their error. (Romans 1:26-27)*

You must remember in all issues relative to God, that people will come up with all kinds of rationalizations to justify their own sinful behavior even if they believe in God. Others will do whatever they want not giving God a second thought, disavowing His existence. Remember that God exists! He has always existed, and He always will exist. The fact that people don't believe in God, does not minimize His existence. The same is true of the Lord Jesus. By the way, they don't need people to believe in them. The Father, Son and Holy Spirit want people to believe in them, but it doesn't change anything about them if people don't believe. The bottom line, however, is this:

> *This will happen when the Lord Jesus is revealed from heaven in blazing fire with his powerful angels. He will punish those who do not know God and do not obey the gospel of our Lord Jesus. They will be punished with everlasting destruction and shut out from the presence of the Lord and from the glory of his might on the day he comes to be glorified in his holy people and to be marveled at among all those who have believed. (2 Thessalonians 1:7-10)*

But, please realize and understand that Christians do NOT hate homosexuals. This idea and notion has been promoted for a long time by many people. If they can convince themselves that Christians hate homosexuals, or anyone for that matter, then they believe that their reasoning that God is unfair and unjust nullifies his existence. They believe incorrectly that a loving God would never be against any two-people loving each other, and making a marriage commitment to each other regardless of their sex. Hence, they believe that their behavior is justifiable, because there is now no authoritative being. Anyway, the point is that Christians love all people including those who practice homosexuality. It is just that Christians take a stand against anything that God denotes as sinful behavior. Therefore, Christians attempt to persuade people to repent of their sinful lifestyles.

Understanding Money

Watch your heart when it comes to money! Money has the ability to shipwreck your faith. It has the ability to take you in directions that you shouldn't go. To do things that you shouldn't do, and to corrupt your character. Jesus and the apostles spoke and wrote about money a lot. Here is what Jesus said about money while giving His Sermon on the Mount:

> *"No one can serve two masters. Either you will hate the one and love the other, or you will be devoted to the one and despise the other. You cannot serve both God and money. (Matthew 6:24)*

Please heed these words, and all the words, of Jesus. Therefore, learn to keep money in its proper place. Love God more than money. Love God more than money. One more time, love God more than money! Say it often and write it into your heart. Love God more than money! Trust me, you can never say this to yourself, or anyone else, too much. The apostle Paul addressed the fact that the love of money is at issue for all people, including Christians.

> *For the love of money is a root of all kinds of evil. Some people, eager for money, have wandered from the faith and pierced themselves with many griefs. (1 Timothy 6:10)*

Realize that in the quest for money you may lose yourself. You may sacrifice priceless possessions (i.e. relationships) and your well-being in your quest. Don't ever let that happen.

Give yourself over to God, and in so doing become a servant of God not of money. As Jesus has said, you cannot do both. Learn to understand that money is a tool. And remember that any tool is only as good as the person whom holds it. So, be wise with the money that God provides to you. And always remember that whatever money you have, you have because God has given it to you. Therefore, honor God with your money and give a portion back to God as He commands.

> *Each of you should give what you have decided in your heart to give, not reluctantly or under compulsion, for God loves a cheerful giver. (2 Corinthians 9:7)*

Make sure that you are controlling your money. Your money should not control you. Understand that money is not evil. Money is an inanimate object. It holds no value to God in and of itself. The value to God has to do with what you do with your money. The value to God comes into play when you use it for the glory of God.

Alcohol and Drug Abuse

Using alcohol and drugs as a form of entertainment, or to enhance an entertainment experience is simply a bad idea. So, burn this into your mind and memory as soon as possible.

Learn to go against the grain, against what most people do. Learn to do things in accordance with the will of God. That's right, learn to do things God's way! Do not adapt to, nor take on the behavior of worldly people. Remember this:

> *Do not conform to the pattern of this world, but be transformed by the renewing of your mind. Then you will be able to test and approve what God's will is—his good, pleasing and perfect will. (Romans 12:2).*

As I write this, our country is suffering from an opioid addiction epidemic. Drugs are pouring over the borders at an alarming rate. People of all ages, and of all walks of life are becoming addicted. Many will die from an overdose. I have seen more than my share of this problem. Steer clear and keep away from any form of alcohol and drug abuse. Once you have an addiction, any type of addiction, it can be very difficult to break away! The best way to stop an addiction, is to never develop an addiction. And remember this, it only takes one bad decision. One momentary lapse of judgment. One seemingly innocent trial. Then, bam, before you know it; you're hooked. And these days with the development of synthetic drugs one time can be the last time. Many people die from taking a synthetic once. Don't become a statistic. Don't put your parents, family and friends through the pain of planning and attending your funeral, or the funeral of someone else who died because of something you did. Now, I know that you may be thinking, "Come on Pop-Pop. Aren't you being a little over dramatic?" Well, I can assure you that I am not. These are very real and possible realities for anyone that takes drugs or drinks alcohol, even once. One of Newton's laws of motion states that: "For every action, there is an equal and opposite reaction." This is also true with life. Our actions have consequences. Consequences aren't all bad. There are good and bad consequences. A consequence is, by definition, a reaction to an action. Remember that your actions have consequences; whether they are good or bad is up to you. Please make godly choices!

I have lost a number of friends that experimented with either drugs or alcohol, or both. I have done funeral services for families that have lost loved ones due to the use of drugs, or alcohol or both. These were some of the saddest times of my ministry. Remember that the choices that you make are not only about you. Far from it, the choices that you make have the potential to impact the lives of everyone who loves and/or knows you. Therefore, you have a tremendous responsibility.

In the late 1980's, the First Lady at the time, Nancy Reagan began a campaign against drug abuse. The tag line was, "Just say No to drugs!" It was very popular, and experienced wide recognition. People all over the place were saying, "Just say No to drugs!"

But something has happened! Our government over the years has grown less enthusiastic with the notion of preventing drug addiction, and more comfortable with treating the cases of addiction that are occurring. Now, with the election of Donald J. Trump as the President of the United States of America in 2016 things may change. President Trump seems committed to fighting against the massive influx of drugs that are pouring into the country on a daily basis. I am not intending for this to be a political writing in any way. It's just that our children are dying needless deaths, and someone needs to do something. I see President Trump as being the one who is willing to do what needs to be done. Please pray for our President, whoever they are. Pray for all the leaders of our country. Pray for them if they are Republican. Pray for them if they are Democratic. Pray for them if they are men. Pray for them if they are women. Pray, pray, pray! Our country is dependent upon your prayers.

Finally, remember and understand that resisting the advances of the devil (Satan) are difficult enough when sober. So, doing anything that impairs your judgment and decision-making ability is detrimental. Peter reminds Christians everywhere:

> *Be alert and of sober mind. Your enemy the devil prowls around like a roaring lion looking for someone to devour. (1 Peter 5:8)*

Do not make yourself an easy target for the devil. Do all that you can to keep your mind sharp, and your senses keen. Be on-guard against the schemes of the devil, and the people he will use to trip you up.

Stay sober. Stay strong. Stay in and with the Lord!

God Tests, and Satan Tempts

Similarly, to the issue of free will, the notions of God testing people while Satan tempts people can be quite confusing. In this section I hope to clear up any confusion you may have on these matters.

Well, let's begin in the beginning. That is let's begin with the fall of man, due to the temptations of the devil (Satan). Here's what the Bible reveals to us:

> *Now the serpent was more crafty than any of the*
> *wild animals the LORD God had made. He said*
> *to the woman, "Did God really say, 'You must*
> *not eat from any tree in the garden'?"*
> *The woman said to the serpent, "We may eat*
> *fruit from the trees in the garden, but God did*
> *say, 'You must not eat fruit from the tree that*
> *is in the middle of the garden, and you must not*
> *touch it, or you will die.'"*
> *You will not certainly die," the serpent said to*
> *the woman. "For God knows that when you eat*
> *from it your eyes will be opened, and you will*
> *be like God, knowing good and evil." (Genesis*
> *3:1-5)*

Right here we see the devil doing one of the things he does best, putting a temptation before people. Unfortunately, in this case Eve fell to the temptation of the devil. Not only that, but in this case the devil persuades Eve to think impure thoughts about God. He convinces her to believe that God was holding out on her. That God did not want her to be god-like. Well Satan's persuasions took root, and she gave-in to the temptation.

In another case, Jesus was severely tempted by the devil. This took place immediately after Jesus was baptized by John the Baptist (not to be confused with the apostle John). The gospel of Matthew tells us that Jesus was led by the Spirit into the wilderness to be tempted by the devil. (Matthew 4:1)

In these temptations, the devil is referred to as being the tempter. Paul, also makes reference to the devil as being the tempter.

So, the point here is that when you are being tempted understand that it is Satan (the devil) putting the temptation before you. How you respond is up to you! Remember this Scripture, and commit it to memory:

> *No temptation has overtaken you except what is common to mankind. And God is faithful; he will not let you be tempted beyond what you can bear. But when you are tempted, he will also provide a way out so that you can endure it. (1 Corinthians 10:13)*

Learn to respond to the faithfulness of God, and take the way out that God provides.

Don't ever blame God for the temptations that you experience. You and you alone are responsible for the temptations that you experience. That's right, you are responsible. I know, that's hard to hear. Want proof? Well, here you are:

> *When tempted, no one should say, "God is tempting me." For God cannot be tempted by evil, nor does he tempt anyone; but each person is tempted when they are dragged away by their own evil desire and enticed. (James 1:13-14)*

Satan puts temptations before you based on the evil desires that reside within you. How does he know what they are, you may ask? Well, Satan or other forces of evil have been watching you at specific times. They have had the luxury of trial and error over time. They have been able to see how you react to specific temptations. Therefore, they have learned what works and what doesn't. And they have become very efficient.

God loves you, and He would never tempt you to sin. Even if He could, He wouldn't. God does not want you to sin, so He would never entice you to commit any type of sin. That's what Satan does. So, then, what is God's role on such issues? Well, God's role is that He tests us at times. He often allows the temptations of Satan to serve as a testing ground. We see this in the temptations placed before Job. In the first few chapters of Job, we see that Satan gets permission, from God, to tempt Job a number of times. That's good news for all of us. It proves that God is in control of everything, including what Satan does to us. This is and must be the case, otherwise God would not be able to make the promise of providing a way out during the times of temptation. These temptations also serve as tests allowed by God. You may see this as a small point, but I encourage you to see its criticality. If you don't have the correct mindset, you may begin to see God in an unfavorable light. You may fall to the temptation to blame God, when you face temptation. This will have a multitude of negative effects, which is exactly what Satan wants. So, remember that God tests, and Satan tempts.

There are very specific purposes for God testing you. One of them is that in a test, God shows you where your faith really is, compared to where you thought it was. All through the Bible we see God testing people. Some come through with flying colors, while others fail miserably. Success is based on faith. Success is based on trust. Success is based on your love for God. Success is based on your knowledge of God's Word, and your ability to apply it in specific situations. So, study the temptations of Jesus in Matthew Chapter 4. Learn how to do what Jesus did, and you will be successful in fighting through temptations!

Conclusion

Well, that does it! I have said all that have to say for this book. Please excuse any errors that appear in this book, as it has been a bit challenging to edit well considering the way that I have been feeling. Please know, however, that working on this book has been both a labor of love and a blessing in many ways. On the many sleepless nights that I have had, I have rested in writing. On the many occasions that I have experienced pain, writing has been a welcomed distraction. With the ongoing sadness that I have about not being here for you (my grandchildren), writing this book has helped to fill a tremendous void. I thank God for this accomplishment, and I hope that He is pleased with all that I have had to say about Him!

I hope and pray that you continue to find this material helpful in your walk with the Lord Jesus. I hope and pray that you continue to grow in your understanding of God's love, grace and mercy. I hope and pray that you become a Christian, that you stay a Christian, that your mate is a Christian and that you raise your children (if God blesses you with them) to become Christians as well.

I look forward to seeing you on the other side!

Finally, always remember the following passage:

> *Do not love the world or anything in the world.*
> *If anyone loves the world, love for the Father is*
> *not in them. For everything in the world—the*

lust of the flesh, the lust of the eyes, and the pride of life—comes not from the Father but from the world. The world and its desires pass away, but whoever does the will of God lives forever. (1 John 2:15-17)

I love you and I thank God For you!

> All My Love - In Christ,
> Pop-Pop

CPSIA information can be obtained
at www.ICGtesting.com
Printed in the USA
LVOW13s0830110318
569446LV00009B/285/P